"Lee Salz has cracked the code on what makes first meetings truly effective. *The First Meeting Differentiator* doesn't just change the way you approach first meetings—it changes the way prospects engage with you. If you're tired of first meetings that go nowhere, read this book and turn them into deal-winning conversations."

—CARYN KOPP,
Chief Door Opener at Kopp Consulting
and founder of the Door Opener Service

"I have known Lee for many years, and he is a true sales guru. *The First Meeting Differentiator* is a must-read. It takes the fear out of first meetings by giving you a step-by-step roadmap to success."

—DR. TONY ALESSANDRA,
author of *Non-Manipulative Selling*
and *The Platinum Rule for DISC Sales Mastery*

"Sales does not have a closing problem; sales has an opening problem. If we're serious about helping customers, we have to up our first meeting game. Lee shows us the way to do just that in *The First Meeting Differentiator*. He presents a comprehensive strategy to create a first-meeting experience that sets the journey to close more deals. If you're serious about closing more business than ever before, read this book!"

—MARK HUNTER,
The Sales Hunter and author of *A Mind for Sales*

"*The First Meeting Differentiator* is genius: An inspiring deep dive into the purpose and psychology of a first meeting, first dissecting what is usually wrong, then putting together in great detail how to do it better. As Lee puts it, it's 'a journey to create masterful consultations.' Reads like a novel; you cannot put it down."

—BARBARA WEAVER,
Principal of Strategic Writing Service

"Too many salespeople obsess over getting meetings, which is a salesperson-focused approach. Then, opportunities are wasted with a robotic-discovery approach. *The First Meeting Differentiator* doesn't relabel discovery; it replaces it with a human other-focused strategy that turns first meetings into value-packed, consultative conversations that spark action and drive deals forward. Engaging buyer emotions, crafting effective questions, and developing compelling stories (rather than boring features and benefit lectures), this book has everything you need to develop the pipeline you've always wanted. If you've ever struggled to turn first meetings into meaningful business conversations that move the buying process forward, this book provides a blueprint you can apply in real time."

—ART SOBCZAK,
author of *Smart Calling: Eliminate the Fear,*
Failure, and Rejection from Cold Calling

"Why has this book not been written before? It's a question I asked myself over and over again as I read it. The value drips off the pages at every turn, from understanding the buyer's perspective to effective preparation, structure, and personalization. For anyone in sales, this book will sharpen your approach to first meetings and put you in a better position to move deals forward. Lee once again sets up salespeople for success, creating an essential book of tools."

—SIMON HARES,
founder and Managing Director of SerialTrainer7

"*The First Meeting Differentiator* is one of the most innovative, unique, and game-changing books I have read in years. Lee shares his wisdom and expertise to demystify the most critical parts of the sales process—the first meeting. In this powerful read, he gives you a step-by-step game plan that will transform your first meetings and results!"

—MERIDITH ELLIOTT POWELL,
Business Growth Strategist, Hall of Fame speaker,
and bestselling author of *Thrive: Strategies to Turn*
Uncertainty into Competitive Advantage

"*The First Meeting Differentiator* is a must-read for anyone serious about sales. Lee masterfully shifts the first meeting from a scripted interrogation into a meaningful, client-centric consultation that builds trust and fuels deal momentum. This book is packed with real strategies that will help you close more deals faster."

—**BRANDON BORNANCIN,**
CEO of Seamless.AI
and bestselling author of *Whatever It Takes*

"Lee has once again delivered a game-changing masterpiece for sales professionals. *The First Meeting Differentiator* doesn't just challenge conventional thinking—it completely transforms how you approach the most critical moment in the sales process: the first meeting. Lee changes the game from tired discovery checklists to dynamic, value-driven consultations that resonate with prospects. This book has real-world strategies, stories, and practical tools that help you build trust fast, qualify smarter, and keep deals moving forward. If you're ready to stop losing deals in the first meeting and start building unstoppable momentum from the first handshake, this book is your new flight plan."

—**DAVE SANDERSON,**
speaker, author, and philanthropist

"The title alone—*The First Meeting Differentiator*—grabs any sales pro's attention. After all, your income hinges on the impression you make in that very first conversation. And then you see the name: Salz. Lee Salz. A master of sales strategy whose work I've followed for over fifteen years. This book is classic Salz—original thinking and real-world tactics that elevate your game. Chapter 5's focus on Empathetic Expertise reshaped how I think about emotional intelligence in sales. And chapter 8's Consultation Cliffhangers gave me a fresh, strategic way to keep deals moving forward. Whether you're an individual rep looking to sharpen your skills or a leader looking to boost your team's performance, this book has it all!"

—**DAN SEIDMAN OF GOT INFLUENCE,**
author of *The Ultimate Guide to Sales Training*

"There is a saying, 'When the student is ready, the teacher appears,' and when it comes to anything that Lee Salz writes, I am always a student. His new book has scored three home runs for me. First, it has depth. In a world of thought repeaters, his thought leadership shines with fresh ideas and new ways of looking at the sales conversation. Second, it is modern. He has incorporated AI in a practical and relevant way, making sense for any salesperson willing to do the work. Third, it is balanced. He has integrated logic and emotion in an extremely balanced way, which, for me, is important in the world we are in now."

—**BERNADETTE MCCLELLAND,**
CEO of the Sales Leadership Academy

"An effective first meeting is crucial. Without it, there's no opportunity for a second. In *The First Meeting Differentiator*, Lee Salz provides essential insights into the 'what' and 'how' of organizing a successful initial encounter. This book is indispensable, offering practical steps every sales professional needs to follow to ensure progress from the first meeting to the next."

—**THOMAS J. WILLIAMS,**
founder and chairman of Strategic Dynamics Inc.

"Reps always say, 'If I could just get the meeting . . .' but then fall short once they do. The average success rate for a salesperson advancing a deal from first call to closed deal is painfully low—just 15 percent. *The First Meeting Differentiator* moves that success needle by providing sales professionals with a proven initial-meeting strategy, framework, and game plan that lays the foundation for landing accounts. It puts an end to the discovery mindset and shifts to a consultation mindset that propels deals forward. This book will transform how you approach first meetings. Read it with a highlighter handy. You're going to need it!"

—**BRYNNE TILLMAN,**
co-author of *The LinkedIn Edge* and
Prompt Writing Made Easy

"As someone who has studied, taught, and obsessed over discovery calls for fifteen-plus years, I thought I'd seen it all—until I read *The First Meeting Differentiator*. Lee Salz doesn't just rethink the first meeting— he reinvents it. This book delivers a masterclass in turning 'just another sales call' into a high-value consultation that builds trust, sparks momentum, and makes every opportunity much more likely to close."

—DAVID NEWMAN,
bestselling author of *Do It! Marketing* and *Do It! Selling*

"As someone who teaches salespeople how to prepare for sales interactions, I'm thrilled there's finally a book dedicated to mastering the first meeting. *The First Meeting Differentiator* isn't just another sales book—it's a game-changing guide packed with real-world stories and hands-on workshops that help salespeople craft a winning first-meeting strategy. If you want a stronger pipeline and higher close rates, this book is a must-read!"

—SAM RICHTER,
CSP, CPAE, Professional Speaker Hall of Fame,
bestselling author, and founder of Intel Engine.ai

"B2B buyers don't have time for salespeople who don't bring value. If you're not bringing value from the first meeting, you're out. Lee Salz delivers exactly what sales professionals need to rise above the noise: a strategy built on insights, ideas, and impact. Lee Salz, the expert on sales differentiation, struck a chord with this book. *The First Meeting Differentiator* is timely, practical, and essential for anyone serious about earning business in today's market."

—FRED DIAMOND,
founder of the Institute for Effective Professional Selling

"Deals are won or lost in the first meeting—period. In *The First Meeting Differentiator*, Lee hands you the game plan to turn that conversation into a trust-building, deal-driving advantage. If you're serious about growing revenue, this isn't optional reading—it's essential."

—DARRELL AMY,
author of *Revenue Growth Engine* and *The Business Owner's Guide to Maximize Business Valuation*

"*The First Meeting Differentiator* is a game-changing resource for sales professionals. This book provides a step-by-step framework to transform initial meetings into dynamic consultations that deliver meaningful value. If you want to strengthen your pipeline, close deals faster, and stand out from all the other salespeople, this book is an essential addition to your sales library. Don't just read this book, implement it."

—LARRY LEVINE,
author of *Selling from the Heart*
and *Selling in a Post-Trust World*

"Most sales meetings feel like an interrogation or mechanical. Lee shows you how to turn the first meeting into an authentic, human conversation that builds trust, creates value, and respects the buyer's buying process. It's not only about asking better questions. It's about showing up differently. *The First Meeting Differentiator* is your guide to transforming mundane meetings into meaningful relationships. Simple, practical, and real, this book changes the way you sell from the very first hello."

—KEITH ROSEN,
CEO of Profit Builders and author of
Coaching Salespeople Into Sales Champions

"This book is a masterclass in turning conversations into conversions, packed with strategy, real-world stories, and tactical brilliance. As someone who believes salespeople should be courageously bold, I found the emphasis on bringing insight and empathy to the table incredibly powerful, especially the section on Empathetic Expertise."

—ANDREA WALTZ,
co-author of *Go for No!*

"I learn something new from Lee every time I read his content. And I'm already selling more based on his advice in *The First Meeting Differentiator*. If you need more pipeline and want to close more deals, read this book ASAP."

—MATT HEINZ,
founder and president of Heinz Marketing Inc.

"I've read over 500 sales and marketing books authored by over 360 authors whom I interviewed for *The Marketing Book Podcast*. Lee Salz is one of my favorite authors. His books are very different, surprisingly effective, and written for people who don't particularly enjoy reading business books. I strongly recommend reading *The First Meeting Differentiator* if you or your sales team need to dramatically differentiate yourself from the competition and start selling more immediately."

—DOUGLAS BURDETT,
host of *The Marketing Book Podcast*

"Finally—a book that zeroes in on the moment that makes or breaks a sale: the first meeting. *The First Meeting Differentiator* delivers a comprehensive strategy for turning that crucial conversation into your competitive edge. If you want to stand out and position yourself to win the deal, this is your playbook!"

—RON KARR,
author of *The Velocity Mindset*® and the
bestselling *Lead, Sell, or Get Out of the Way!*

"First impressions happen in moments, not minutes, when you are selling. Lee has cracked the code to create a cadence of those key moments during a first meeting to capture your prospect's interest and support. Lee has set out a clear set of instructions for the magic moments to happen. If you sell big sales, this approach to the first meeting will give you a great advantage."

—TOM SEARCY,
founder of Hunt Big Sales and a
Top 10 Global Sales Guru

"I highly recommend anything Lee touches, as he understands that sales is nothing other than building bridges of trust with people. That's exactly what this book will help you to do—build bridges of trust."

—ANTARCTIC MIKE

"Forget everything you think you know about first meetings—this book is the game-changer. *The First Meeting Differentiator* is more than a sales guide; it's a masterclass in human connection disguised as a business book. Lee shifts the first meeting from interrogation to consultation, from 'me-focused' discovery to 'you-focused' magic. Imagine walking out of every first meeting with your prospect not just interested but excited, not just listening but leaning in. If your deals stall before they start, Lee gives you the ignition key. This book isn't just about winning more deals—it's about redefining how selling feels. Read it, use it, and watch 'maybe' turn into an enthusiastic 'yes.'"

—**GERHARD GSCHWANDTNER,**
CEO of Selling Power

"Having read all of Lee's books, I can confidently say *The First Meeting Differentiator* is his most powerful work yet. Lee masterfully shifts the sales conversation from self-focused pitching to client-centered consultation—exactly the transformation today's sales professionals need. Each of his books has delivered massive value to my growth and my clients, but this one raises the bar yet again. If you're serious about earning trust and setting the stage for success from the very first meeting, this is the playbook. Get this book—it will transform the way you sell forever!"

—**JOE CRISARA,**
America's Service Sales Coach of ServiceMVP.com

"I've followed Lee for years—his insights always challenge the status quo. *The First Meeting Differentiator* is a true game-changer. While others obsess over closing, Lee shows that the real win happens in the first meeting. With a smart shift from 'discovery' to 'consultation,' this book delivers both strategy and practical tools to help you dominate from the start."

—**LAHAT TZVI,**
CEO of Tfisot

"If your first meetings aren't leading to second meetings, you need this book. Lee gives you the blueprint to shift from just 'asking questions' to delivering real value, making your first meeting the start of a winning relationship, not a wasted opportunity."

—**DIANE HELBIG,**
award-winning author, speaker, and trainer

"Lee has done it again! *The First Meeting Differentiator* delivers a message the way only Lee can—clear, concise, and insightful. In a sales world focused on just getting to the first meeting, this book guides you on what to do when you book the meeting. First impressions are too important to fumble; after reading this, you'll carry the sale to the end zone."

—**SKIP WILLCOX,**
founder of Kairos Sales Group

"Lee gets to the heart of what makes first meetings matter. *The First Meeting Differentiator* is packed with insights that challenge outdated habits and replace them with a smarter, more intentional approach to selling. It is a thoughtful, practical guide to transforming first meetings into conversations that spark real interest and build genuine momentum. He reminds us that it's not about saying everything—it's about saying the right things in a way that sparks curiosity and earns the next conversation. If you're leading a team and want to create a more repeatable, buyer-centered, first-meeting process, this book delivers."

—**DENISE HARRISON,**
president/CEO of Spex, Inc., and a
Strategic Planning and Execution Expert

"Lee Salz delivers a game-changing blueprint that transforms the first meeting into a value-packed consultation, arming sales professionals with the mindset, strategy, and tools to build trust, differentiate effectively, and close more deals without sacrificing price."

—**MARY KELLY,**
author of *Stop Procrastinating Tomorrow*

"*The First Meeting Differentiator* takes sales strategy to a whole new level, redefining how to approach first meetings for maximum impact. Lee introduces the game-changing concept of Empathetic Expertise™— the key to positioning yourself as a trusted consultant rather than just another salesperson. Too many first meetings fail because salespeople rush to prescribe solutions before truly diagnosing the client's needs. With 75 percent of first sales calls never leading to a second, this book is the ultimate playbook for earning trust, igniting engagement, and securing the next step. If you want to turn first meetings into lasting opportunities, this is a must-read!"

—STU SCHLACKMAN,
member of the Top 30 Global Sales Gurus and
past president of the National Speakers
Association-North Texas chapter

"Lee doesn't just reshape the first meeting—he revolutionizes it. In a world where buyers crave value and insight from the very first conversation, Lee's consultative approach equips sales teams with a repeatable framework to stand out and win more deals at the right price. If you're a sales leader looking to boost win rates and differentiate your team, this book is your new secret weapon—and bringing Lee in to speak will make it real for your people."

—MERIT KAHN,
CSP, Emotional Intelligence Expert,
and CEO of SELLect Sales Development

"Lee has done it again with *The First Meeting Differentiator*! Everyone knows the first meeting is crucial, but few know how to truly master it—until now. Lee provides game-changing insights on preparation, powerful questions to ask, and real-world examples to bring his methods to life. Most importantly, he shows you how to close the first meeting in a way that propels deals forward. If you want to turn first meetings into winning opportunities, this book is a must-read!"

—JIM JOHNSON,
Hall of Fame retired high school basketball
coach, motivational speaker, and author

"Lee is fantastic at identifying key points, which can deliver impactful results as soon as they are put into practice. For example, the Target Client Profile is a wonderful example of putting theory to practical use. It is a simple way to ensure you are investing your time—rather than spending your time—on opportunities you can win at the prices you want. *The First Meeting Differentiator* is essential reading for anyone in sales or who leads a salesforce."

—VINCE BURRUANO,
Sales and Leadership Success Coach

"Lee's evolution of discovery to a first-meeting consultation is so masterful that it surprised even me, and I've known him for years. This is modern consultative selling at its finest. If you're still stuck in traditional 'discovery,' *The First Meeting Differentiator* will elevate your approach to a higher level of sales effectiveness that lays the foundation for successful opportunity management."

—MIKE KUNKLE,
VP of Sales Effectiveness Services at SPARXiQ
and author of *The Building Blocks of Sales Enablement*

"There is nothing more important than the first meeting. Lee Salz will ensure you get the best start."

—ANTHONY IANNARINO,
author of *Elite Sales Strategies*

"Many deals are won or lost in the first meeting, so why aren't more salespeople mastering this critical moment? Lee Salz delivers a game-changing approach to turning first meetings into competitive advantages. If you want to win more deals at the prices you want, it is imperative you read this book."

—RON HUBSHER,
author of *Closing Time:*
The 7 Immutable Laws of Sales Negotiation

"Most sales books tell you what to do. Lee finally shows you how. From the very first question—"What do you know, that decision influencers don't know, but need to know now?"—you'll feel the shift. Lee hands both new reps and seasoned pros a step-by-step game plan to turn first meetings into meaningful conversations (you know, the kind that actually lead to next steps). Packed with how-to gold, story-driven strategies, and practical tools, this book doesn't just sit on your shelf—it changes the way you sell."

—LYNN HIDY,
UpYourTeleSales, Inside Sales Consultant,
mastermind facilitator, and trainer

"One of the most valuable things this book offers is a clear, actionable structure for showing up fully prepared to a first sales meeting. Lee Salz doesn't just preach about being different—he gives you a practical framework to make a memorable impression by treating the first meeting like a true consultation, not a fishing expedition."

—BARRY TRAILER,
co-founder of Sales Mastery

"Want to stand out in the vital first meeting with a prospect? Add value first. How can you do that? Read this book!"

—PHIL GERBYSHAK,
Sales Enablement Expert and veteran sales podcaster

"*The First Meeting Differentiator* turns the table on discovery calls. From the prospect's perspective, a discovery call is where the salesperson peppers them with questions and offers little value. Lee shows you how to transform the discovery call into a valuable consultation. The consultation is so beneficial that the prospect wants more! Read the wisdom between these pages and transform your discovery calls!"

—ANDY MILLER,
CEO of Big Swift Kick and
international bestselling author

"*The First Meeting Differentiator* is a book that will transform your sales productivity. It's a new, refreshing, and effective way to align yourself with customers and achieve sustained sales success. I've always been a Lee Salz fan. This book adds to his reputation as a top-notch sales coach."

—**MAX CATES,**
Sales Management Consultant and author
of the new book *4 Steps to Supercharged Sales Teams*

"*The First Meeting Differentiator* isn't just another sales book; it's a playbook for sellers who want to lead with insight, build real trust, and earn the second meeting. Lee exposes the tired old 'discovery call' mindset and replaces it with a powerful, buyer-centric approach rooted in relevance, value, and expertise. He provides a leading-edge approach required to win when selling and partnering with the buyer of today and the future. If you want to stop sounding like every other rep and start winning bigger deals, start here."

—**SHANE GIBSON,**
keynote speaker and sales author

"*The First Meeting Differentiator* is the playbook sales pros have been waiting for. Lee changes outdated discovery calls to a consultative approach that drives deal momentum from the first conversation. Insightful. Practical. A must-read."

—**STEVEN ROSEN,**
Top Executive Coach 2025, and founder
and Executive Coach of STAR Results

"Too many salespeople think the first meeting is just about gathering intel; Lee Salz proves it's about delivering value. This book will change how you think about first meetings and, more importantly, how your prospects experience them. Read it, apply it, and watch your sales soar."

—**MATTHEW POLLARD,**
bestselling author of the Introvert's Edge series

"*The First Meeting Differentiator* isn't just another sales book—it's a game plan for turning first meetings into deal-winning opportunities. Lee tears down the outdated 'discovery meeting' approach and replaces it with a powerful, value-driven consultation strategy. This book arms sales professionals with the tools to engage prospects, establish expertise, and differentiate from the competition right from the start. If you're serious about winning more deals at the prices you want, this is the blueprint you've been waiting for."

—PASCAL FINETTE,
founder and CEO of radical

"The sales profession talks a lot about consultative selling, but too few sales reps actually practice it. In *The First Meeting Differentiator*, Lee shows you how to prove your consultative worth during the all-important first meeting with a prospect. Contrary to popular belief, the first meeting is more than a discovery session; it's an impactful conversation that sets the tone for everything to follow. As the old saying goes, you only have one chance to make a good first impression—and you only get one first meeting."

—JEFF BEALS,
author of *Self Marketing Power* and *Selling Saturdays*

"There's so much to love about this book. It doesn't offer shortcuts; it offers real, impactful strategies. Some salespeople may shy away because it requires effort and intention—and that's exactly why it works. Lee lays out a practical, high-impact approach that transforms first meetings into true differentiators. If you're willing to do the work, this book gives you a serious edge."

—FRED COPESTAKE,
bestselling author of *Selling Through Partnering Skills*, *Hybrid Selling*, and *Ethical Selling*

"To be the best, learn from the best—and Lee Salz is one of the best in sales. *The First Meeting Differentiator* is packed with masterful strategies to turn first meetings into real opportunities. If you're struggling to capture a prospect's interest, the sale will never happen. This book gives you the blueprint to stand out, engage decision-makers, and set the stage for winning more business. A must-read for anyone serious about sales success!"

—ELINOR STUTZ,
international bestselling author of
Nice Girls DO Get the Sale

"When I read chapter 5, I was blown away—it struck a deep chord. This chapter isn't just about sales; it's about truly understanding and connecting with prospects on a deep level. I rarely recommend books, but *The First Meeting Differentiator* is an absolute must-read. If you want to transform your sales approach and drive game-changing revenue, get this book and put its strategies into action!"

—PATRICK TINNEY,
Canada's Sales and Negotiation Rainmaker
and four-time sales book author

"When Lee asked for a book review quote for *The First Meeting Differentiator*, my knee-jerk reaction was, 'All meetings have to be differentiated; why focus on the first?' After reading Lee's outstanding book, I was reminded that we never get the second, third, and other meetings without a fantastic first one.

—DAVE BROCK,
author of *Sales Manager Survival Guide* and CEO of Partners In EXCELLENCE

"I agree with Lee—traditional discovery meetings are not only ineffective, they're counterproductive. Lee's insights and techniques will help you change how you think about first meetings and enable you to meet your buyers where they are, leading to better conversations and more sales."

—CAROLE MAHONEY,
author of *Buyer First*

"When salespeople struggle to close deals, the real problem isn't closing—it's opening. Without a strong first meeting, there's no foundation for success. *The First Meeting Differentiator* delivers a game-changing playbook to captivate prospects, build meaningful connections, and set the stage for winning more deals. If you're in sales, this book isn't optional—it's essential!"

—JEFF BAJOREK,
co-host of the podcast *Rethink The Way You Sell*

"Your first meeting isn't about pitching. It's about positioning yourself as an empathetic consultant. Lee shows you how to rethink your mindset, questions, and conversation to focus entirely on your prospect. Thought-provoking conversations uncover stronger opportunities, make you stand out from the start, and leave prospects clamoring to work with you. A sharp, practical guide every sales professional should read."

—KENDRA LEE,
president of KLA Group and
author of *The Sales Magnet*

"Lee set the bar high with *Sell Different!* and *Sales Differentiation*, and *The First Meeting Differentiator* clears it with room to spare. The first sales interaction is make-or-break, yet most reps wing it with no strategy. Lee shows you how to engage deeper, create authentic dialogue, and turn first meetings into second ones. The whole book is great—especially chapters 6, 7, and 8. Game-changers!"

—KELLY RIGGS,
founder of Business LockerRoom, Inc.

"So many sales books are nothing but unproven theory, but not this one! We worked with Lee to develop our sales playbook based on the strategy presented in *The First Meeting Differentiator*. The result? We are closing more sales and earning more happy customers. Just wait until you read the chapter on Empathetic Expertise! It's a game-changer!"

—SCOT NICHOLS,
Director of Sales at Bedrock Quartz

"Follow the advice in *The First Meeting Differentiator* and ROCK your first meetings with prospects! Sales guru Lee Salz has helped our team improve our results by adopting a forensic and consultative mindset. I hope our competitors NEVER read this book!"

—LIZ MCBETH,
CEO and president of Armour Valve

"I hired Lee Salz as my VP of Sales and Marketing over thirty years ago and watched firsthand as *The First Meeting Differentiator* strategy delivered results. We drove record-breaking revenue and sold our company at the prices we wanted. Lee's approach flat-out works."

—ANDREW MACDONALD,
CEO of Consilio

"Most sales books are filled with overused techniques and the buzzwords of the day. But not this one! Our team hit record-breaking sales after working with Lee Salz and applying *The First Meeting Differentiator* strategy. This book is a masterclass in blending proven sales strategies with the emotional drivers behind every buyer's decision. It's practical, powerful, and an absolute must-read for anyone serious about leveling up their sales game."

—JIM WOODRUFF,
CEO of National Powersport Auctions

"*The First Meeting Differentiator* emphasizes the critical importance of the initial sales meeting and challenges the traditional sales-focused discovery approach. It advocates for a 'consultation mindset' that prioritizes delivering immediate value to the prospect, fostering trust, and building deal momentum. This book provides a practical framework and techniques to transform first meetings into engaging, client-centric consultations that effectively qualify leads and ultimately lead to greater sales success. *The First Meeting Differentiator* will go on my bookshelf next to Lee's masterworks *Sales Differentiation* and *Sell Different!* I will be purchasing copies for everyone on my sales team."

—WES AMANN,
VP of Sales at Filterbuy

"I've been a longtime fan of Lee Salz's books, and *The First Meeting Differentiator* raises the bar again. Chapter 4 on preparation is gold—most salespeople aren't ready when they walk into a meeting with a CEO like me. And chapter 6 on Vertical Questions? That alone will level up your sales game. Keep this book close. You'll keep going back to it."

—JERRY L. MILLS,
CEO of B2B CFO® and B2B EXIT®

"*The First Meeting Differentiator* triggered a profound mind shift, dismantling all 'best practice' sales tactics and forever redefining how I engage prospects ('suspects'). Unlike other sales books that lack actionable solutions, this one delivers clear, step-by-step strategies in every chapter, driving immediate impact. As an early-stage deep tech CEO selling to complex organizations, applying Lee's strategies for quick discernment of high-potential opportunities from the tempting mirages (chapter 6), as well as tailored, restrained communication, which pinpoints meaningful value for suspects and keeps them eager for more (chapter 7), has saved valuable time and skyrocketed my pipeline. For anyone leading sales, whether in a start-up or Fortune 500 company, this is a game-changer for driving accelerated growth!"

—LEWIS MOTION,
founder and CEO of WEAV3D Inc.

"Buckle up, revenue warriors! Having seen Lee Salz work his magic for years—turning sales teams into lean, mean, winning machines across all sorts of industries—the strategy presented in *The First Meeting Differentiator* is your secret weapon to drive revenue. Lee has an uncanny knack for slicing through the sales blah-blah and showing you how to make those first conversations not just good but impactful. Forget those awkward 'discovery dances'; Lee has created a client-focused consultation methodology that works. This book will help you make that first meeting feel like a breath of fresh air—a real conversation where buyers feel heard and understood, not just sold to. Don't just read it! Study it!"

—**BARBARA BARNARD,**
seasoned global commercial leader with a track record of
driving significant revenue growth

"Lee has hit another home run with *The First Meeting Differentiator*! It's a much-needed update to the outdated discovery meeting, replacing it with a consultative framework that provides meaningful value and boosts sales effectiveness. I've had global sales teams across multiple countries apply Lee's methodologies for over a decade—with great success. This book will be required reading. I'm excited to see our team put it into practice and the results that follow."

—**DARREN TOOHEY,**
Chief Sales and Customer Officer at CTM

"Lee Salz's first meeting strategy didn't just improve our sales process—it revolutionized it. By shifting our client interactions from transactional to transformational, his differentiation techniques helped my team increase revenue year-over-year by 38 percent . . . during a pandemic! What makes *The First Meeting Differentiator* a game-changer is that these aren't just theories—they're proven, battle-tested strategies that deliver real results. I've seen firsthand how mastering the first meeting can completely change the trajectory of a sales organization. Read this book, embrace the strategy, and watch your sales soar!"

—**DARYL HANCOCK,**
executive leader in the technology field

"*The First Meeting Differentiator* isn't an unimplementable, theory-only sales book. It's a field-tested playbook that works! I know this because Lee coached me on his first-meeting strategy, and it turned my first meetings into momentum-building business consultations. I love how he shares stories in the book to make understanding the concepts easy. Implement Lee's strategy and enjoy the results!"

—GREG D'AMICO,
CEO of Efficience and fourteen-year EO chapter executive

"Discovery is dead—and Lee Salz proves it. *The First Meeting Differentiator* shows why consultative selling isn't optional anymore—it's essential. In a world where time is money, this book teaches you how to deliver value fast, build trust early, and create customer-focused solutions that drive deals forward. If you're still stuck in old-school discovery mode, you're losing opportunities by the minute."

—JOEL BRUNING,
Sales Manager at Vulcraft,
a division of Nucor Corporation

"Great salespeople don't just 'ask better questions'—they create powerful moments that build deal momentum. Lee Salz's *The First Meeting Differentiator* is the ultimate guide to making your first meetings unforgettable. Get this book, implement the strategies, and turn more first meetings into closed deals."

—BRANDON STEINER,
founder of Steiner Sports, and CEO
and founder of CollectibleXchange

"Following the success of Salz's bestsellers *Sales Differentiation* and *Sell Different!*, *The First Meeting Differentiator* is another outstanding new resource that will give your team insights to succeed. It's packed with real-world stories, actionable insights, and hands-on workshops. This book helps you build a first-meeting framework that lays the foundation for your enhanced deal success. I highly recommend it!"

—CHAD SPRETZ,
Vice President of Commercial at Whitmore Manufacturing

"Great salespeople don't just gather information in first meetings—they provide value. *The First Meeting Differentiator* gives you the roadmap to transform those conversations into powerful differentiators that set you apart from the competition."

—**BRUCE BERG,**
president of Berg Consulting Group

"Having worked with Lee twice and read all his books, I think *The First Meeting Differentiator* may be his best work yet. We all know that first meetings make (or break!) any opportunity to help a new client achieve their goals. His insights have personally helped me refine my approach with new clients to be more consultative, thorough, and valuable. I know that Lee's methods work because I've seen them work! If you want to master the art of making a lasting impression from the very first conversation, this is the guide you need. I can't recommend it highly enough!"

—**ROB ALTIERI,**
Managing Partner at Range Tax Advisors

"*The First Meeting Differentiator* is a masterclass in what most sellers get wrong and what elite performers do differently. As someone who's spent my career in complex, relationship-based sales, I found the concept of shifting from discovery to dynamic, value-driven consultation especially powerful. Lee arms sellers with practical strategies that turn your first meeting into a competitive advantage. This book isn't just a differentiator—it's a deal accelerator."

—**CARSON V. HEADY,**
Managing Director at Microsoft
and bestselling author of *Salesman on Fire*

"Lee has identified a crucial sales problem: ineffective first meetings. If you start the sale wrong, it's not going to end well. He illuminates a path for all salespeople to follow that will lead to solving your sales-growth problems."

—**DANIEL BURNS,**
host of *The Sales Problem Podcast*,
sales leader, and ICF-certified performance coach

"In *The First Meeting Differentiator,* Lee Salz presents a comprehensive strategy for structuring first meetings that drive real results. He emphasizes the importance of a well-defined approach—one that fuels differentiation, value creation, and business growth. More than just a methodology, Lee shows how to harness emotion and storytelling to deeply engage prospects and inspire action. His insights are clear, actionable, and rooted in real-world success. This book isn't just about improving prospect meetings—it's about elevating your entire sales game."

—**MARK KNUREK,**
Director of Sales and Marketing
at Mercury Plastics, a Masco business

"Lee Salz has cracked the code on what makes the first meeting truly impactful. *The First Meeting Differentiator* flips traditional sales tactics on their head by transforming discovery sessions into client-centric consultations. As a leader, I know how critical the first impression is—it's where trust is either built or broken. Salz's actionable insights, real-world stories, and step-by-step strategy will equip you to create conversations that leave prospects not just intrigued but eager to move forward. This book is a must-read for anyone serious about accelerating their sales success."

—**BRANDON LEE,**
founder of Fist Bump

"*The First Meeting Differentiator* is a must-read for any sales professional who wants to turn first meetings into real momentum. This book replaces outdated and often unsuccessful discovery calls with value-packed, trust-building consultations that move deals forward. Very practical and immediately useable, this is the first-meeting playbook we've all been waiting for."

—**MIKE MOROZ,**
CEO of Walters Recycling and Refuse, Inc.

"Unlike many sales books that are nothing but theory, this one delivers real-world, actionable strategies that work! How do I know? I've had the privilege of working directly with Lee and implementing the strategies presented in *The First Meeting Differentiator*. My favorite is his Empathetic Expertise™ concept, which has given me the tools to build stronger relationships—and it will do the same for you. If you want a true competitive edge, master every element in this book!"

—**RICHARD MASON,**
owner of GPS Boss

"*The First Meeting Differentiator* redefines the approach to initial sales meetings, transforming them into impactful, client-focused consultations that build trust and ignite interest. Following the acclaim of *Sales Differentiation* and *Sell Different!*, Salz adds another powerful component to your sales strategy. It is an essential read for any salesperson aiming to create strong deal momentum and achieve exceptional success.

—**AARON MCISAAC,**
sales leader, consultant, and entrepreneur

"What sets this book apart from the thousands of other sales books? It's a magical mix of strategic genius and genuine human connection. It doesn't just teach tactics; it transforms your first-meeting mindset. Suddenly, sales isn't about pressure—it's about purpose. Prospects stop being potential dollar signs and start becoming real partners. It's a masterclass focused on getting results."

—**GARY ALEXANDER,**
CEO of IMPROV Learning

"Engagement is the hardest part of sales, and without it, deals fall apart before they even begin. *The First Meeting Differentiator* gives you the tools to capture attention, build trust, and create a rock-solid foundation for winning deals. I've used Lee's strategies—they work, and they'll work for you too!"

—**BRIAN BUCKALEW,**
Vice President of Strategic Sales at Majestic Steel

"In today's sales world, if your first meeting doesn't spark interest and build trust, you're done. *The First Meeting Differentiator* gives you the exact strategy to make that first conversation count—what to say, what to do, and how to earn the right to keep moving forward. Lee doesn't just explain it—he walks you through every step. There's a reason he's known as the best in the business. Nobody does it better."

—VINCENT MELOGRANA,
fifty-five-year sales professional

"Lee nails it with *The First Meeting Differentiator*. This isn't about gimmicks—it's a smart, strategic guide to turning first meetings into meaningful, momentum-building conversations. Packed with real-world insight, this book helps you lead with value, stand out from the start, and set the tone for long-term success. If you're in sales, consulting, or any client-facing role, this is your playbook."

—JIM FREED,
president and CEO of North Country Business Products

"Lee Salz's perspectives on client-centricity are a must-have for the modern world. In *The First Meeting Differentiator*, you'll learn how to run meetings your clients remember and want to take action from. Lee puts you in the headspace of the client and motivates you to be the best version of yourself and the best reflection of your business in your first meetings (and beyond)."

—WILL FRATTINI,
Principal of Enterprise Revenue and Growth at ZoomInfo

"This book is a game-changer for anyone in sales or sales leadership. *The First Meeting Differentiator* reveals how to transform the customer experience into your ultimate competitive advantage. If you're serious about winning more deals and elevating your sales brand, this is a must-read."

—DR. LENITA DAVIS,
Executive Director of the University of
Wisconsin Eau Claire Sales Program
and president of the University
Sales Center Alliance

"*The First Meeting Differentiator* addresses a critically important component in the sales process—the first meeting—which determines whether or not there will be a second meeting. I assure you that my sales team will be required to read this book and implement the strategy."

—**BRIAN WOODBURY**,
Municipal Sales Manager at JH Wright

"*The First Meeting Differentiator* is a game-changer for anyone serious about sales success. In this book, he offers a practical and proven framework for transforming discovery meetings into high-impact consultations. With clear strategies, real-world examples, and powerful tools like Empathetic Expertise™ and Consultation Cliffhangers™, this book is essential for sales professionals who want to stand out and close more deals. I'm excited to share it with our sales students!"

—**DAWN DEETER**,
PhD, professor, J. J. Vanier Distinguished Chair
of Relational Selling and Marketing, and Director
of Kansas State University's National
Strategic Selling Institute

"*The First Meeting Differentiator* is a game-changer for sellers—practical, powerful, and refreshingly human. It helps you earn trust fast, lead with value, and turn first meetings into lasting momentum and trusted long-term relationships. A must-study for all sales professionals."

—**MAREO MCCRACKEN**,
CRO of Movemedical

"In *The First Meeting Differentiator*, Lee doesn't dance around theory. He gives you a real, step-by-step system to turn awkward discovery calls into value-packed consultations that buyers appreciate. The mindset shift he outlines—from 'What can I get from this meeting?' to 'What can I give that's meaningful?'—is a difference-maker. If you want to stop sounding like every other salesperson and start becoming the one buyers remember and trust, read this book."

—**NICOLE GLENN**,
CEO and founder of the Candor Companies

"*The First Meeting Differentiator* presents a winning formula and puts it into a practical, high-impact framework. This book is a must-read for any sales leader and salesperson serious about growth, trust-building, and standing out in every first meeting."

—THEO KRISTORIS,
Managing Director of Leader, Australia's largest PC
manufacturer and privately owned IT distributor

"*The First Meeting Differentiator* throws out the old discovery call playbook and replaces it with a powerful strategy to turn first meetings into deal-making opportunities. This book shows you how to build trust, ignite interest, and set the stage for success. If you've ever left a meeting unsure of what went wrong, this is the book that will show you how to get it right—every time."

—RANDY CHAFFEE,
CEO of Source One Marketing, LLC

"This book is pure fire! I've closed huge deals using Lee's framework, and now he's handing you the playbook. Don't just get meetings; differentiate yourself from the competition, provide meaningful value, and position yourself to win the deal at the prices you want! In the immense swarm of sales books, there is nothing like *The First Meeting Differentiator*."

—RUTHIE NISSIM,
fourteen-year sales professional

"You get one chance to make a first impression with a client, so why do so many salespeople squander this opportunity? Because they've been told to see this meeting through the lens of discovery—an egocentric, limited mindset. *The First Meeting Differentiator* eradicates that outdated approach and presents a comprehensive game plan to turn first meetings into impactful, client-focused consultations that position you to win the account."

—DR. JEFF HOYLE,
professor of professional sales
at Central Michigan University

"If your first meetings aren't leading to second meetings, you need this book. Lee Salz gives you the strategy to shift from just 'asking questions' to delivering real value, making your first meeting the start of a winning relationship, not a wasted opportunity."

—JAMES GRUENING,
co-founder and SVP of Mechdyne Corporation

"*The First Meeting Differentiator* is a must-read for sales professionals. With razor-sharp precision, Lee Salz zeroes in on the most pivotal moment in the buyer-seller journey—the first meeting—providing a comprehensive strategy that transforms initial interactions into deal-driving opportunities. His insights give sellers the edge they need to stand out and boost their win rates. Apply his methods, and you won't just keep up with the competition—you'll leave them behind."

DOUG EDEN,
Chief Revenue Officer of Emtrain

THE FIRST MEETING DIFFERENTIATOR

TRANSFORMING

SALES-FOCUSED **DISCOVERY**

INTO

CLIENT-CENTRIC **CONSULTATIONS**

LEE B. SALZ

HarperCollins
Leadership
An Imprint of HarperCollins

The First Meeting Differentiator
© 2025 by Lee B. Salz

Published by HarperCollins Leadership, an imprint of HarperCollins Focus LLC, 501 Nelson Place, Nashville, TN 37214, USA.

ISBN 978-1-4002-3988-7 (ePub)
ISBN 978-1-4002-3980-1 (HC)

HarperCollins Publishers, Macken House, 39/40 Mayor Street Upper, Dublin 1, Do1 C9W8, Ireland (https://www.harpercollins.com)

Library of Congress Cataloging-in-Publication Data
Library of Congress Cataloging-in-Publication application has been submitted.

Art direction and cover design: Ron Huizinga
Interior Design: Neuwirth & Associates, Inc.

Printed in the United States of America
25 26 27 28 29 LBC 5 4 3 2 1

To my incredible kids, Jamie, Steven, and David

I don't know what I did to deserve such an amazing gift in each of you. Every day, you fill my heart with pride, not just through your accomplishments but in the love and support you show one another. Let nothing stand in the way of pursuing your dreams, because you are capable of more than you can imagine.

To my amazing wife, Sharon

From the moment we met, you have made me a better person in more ways than I can count. Your love, support, and unwavering belief in me inspire me to be the best person I can be. I am forever thankful to walk this journey of life by your side.

To my dad, Joseph Salz
who passed away in December 2022

He left me with a lasting gift—an expression that continues to guide me: Don't just do it; do it right!

To my mom, Myra Salz

Thank you for always being in my corner, cheering me on, and believing in me. Your support means more than words can say!

To my sister, Marlo Salz

I thank the heavens every day for giving me a sister as wonderful as you.

To my in-laws, Paul and Gail Pershes

Thank you for your continued support of my life's pursuits.

CONTENTS

ACKNOWLEDGMENTS

The First Meeting Differentiator would not have been possible without the contributions of many incredible people. I am immensely grateful for their support and involvement in this journey.

- Sharon Salz, my wife and superstar editor

- Steven Salz, my amazing son (you read about him in chapter 1 of *Sell Different!*)

- Marlo Salz, my incredible sister

- Wes Amann, VP of Sales at Filterbuy

- Lisa Chase, twenty-five-year sales professional

- Dawn Deeter, PhD, professor, J. J. Vanier Distinguished Chair of Relational Selling and Marketing, and Director of Kansas State University's National Strategic Selling Institute

- Doug Eden, Chief Revenue Officer, Emtrain

- Rob Fontaine, President, Upstate Door

- Daryl Hancock, Business Consultant

- Richard Mason, owner of GPS Boss

- Aaron McIsaac, sales leader, consultant, and entrepreneur

- Mike Moroz, CEO of Walters Recycling and Refuse, Inc.

- Ruthie Nissim, fourteen-year sales professional

My deepest gratitude to my clients and their sales teams for placing their trust in me and embracing my methodology to *win more deals at the prices you want*®.

A heartfelt thank you to Verne Harnish for contributing a fantastic foreword to *The First Meeting Differentiator*. Your insights add immense value to this book, and I'm truly grateful for your support.

FOREWORD BY VERNE HARNISH

Would someone pay for just meeting with your salesperson? Are they bringing to the table such value in the first meeting that your prospect looks forward to the next meeting (and proposal)?

Success in sales results from a meticulously crafted strategy, precise execution, and an unwavering commitment to understanding your buyers better than they understand themselves. As someone who has spent decades working with business leaders to scale their companies, I've seen a universal truth emerge: *The foundation of every thriving business is built on a deep understanding of its clients and their needs.* In sales, this truth becomes even more critical.

The first meeting—the process of uncovering your buyers' motivations, challenges, and desires—is the cornerstone of effective selling. Yet in many organizations, salespeople struggle to move beyond surface-level interactions. Even worse, they approach the meeting with a discovery mindset that leads to valueless interaction for the buyer rather than, as this presents, a consultation mindset with an emphasis on buyers receiving meaningful value from the interaction.

The message is clear—if you want to differentiate yourself in today's crowded marketplace, you must master the art and science of the first meeting. That's why this book is such an important contribution to the sales world.

In my books *Scaling Up: How a Few Companies Make It . . . and Why the Rest Don't* and *Mastering the Rockefeller Habits*, I've emphasized the importance of scaling businesses through clear strategic focus, operational discipline, and team alignment. But here's the thing: None of those principles can come to life without a robust sales strategy anchored in understanding. Whether you're scaling a start-up or driving growth in a Fortune 500 company, the ability for salespeople to conduct effective first meetings with potential clients is the keystone to unlocking opportunity.

The first meeting isn't just about asking questions; it's about asking the *right* questions. It's about genuinely listening, observing, engaging emotions, and being curious enough to dig deeper. Think of it as peeling back the layers of an onion—each layer reveals more about what drives your buyer's decision. The best salespeople leverage the first meeting to build trust, uncover hidden objections, and position their solution as not just the best choice but the *only* choice.

The pages you're about to dive into are brimming with insights that will help you elevate your sales game. Lee Salz doesn't just talk about what works; he's distilled years of real-world experience into a practical guide that will transform how you think about the first meeting. This book is a masterclass in turning conversations into conversions.

Another aspect that resonates deeply with me is the emphasis this book places on differentiation. In today's hypercompetitive landscape, the ability to stand out is not a luxury; it's a necessity. Buyers have endless choices and are inundated with noise. If you can't articulate how you're different in a way that matters to them, the only conversation you'll have is about price. Lee brilliantly connects the first meeting with his Sales Differentiation® strategies, showing how understanding your buyer's world allows you to position yourself not just as another option but as the ideal partner.

I'm reminded of the adage, "Prescription without diagnosis is malpractice." This is true in medicine, and it's true in sales. Selling without a prescribed first meeting experience is the fastest way to lose credibility and, ultimately, the deal. This book doesn't just explain this principle; it offers actionable tools and techniques to ensure you avoid this pitfall.

Seventy-four percent of buyers choose the salesperson who was first to add value and insight during the buying process. This statistic drives home the importance of mastering the first meeting—it's your opportunity to be that value-driven partner from the start and stand out from the competition.

Whether you're a seasoned sales professional, a team leader, or an entrepreneur looking to elevate your sales game, this book is for you.

So, my recommendation is simple: Read this book. But don't stop there. Highlight and dog-ear pages. Take notes. Most importantly, take action! Incorporate this first meeting strategy into your sales process. Your buyers—and your bottom line—will thank you.

—Verne Harnish
Founder, Entrepreneurs' Organization (EO)
Author of *Start to Scale* and *Scaling Up*

INTRODUCTION

Right now, you're likely asking yourself two questions: *Why did Lee Salz write this book?* And, *Why should I read it?* If you are smiling because that is precisely what you are thinking, you are going to love chapter 5 on Empathetic Expertise™, which dives deep into the art of emotionally connecting with your buyers to energize your deals.

Countless studies confirm what you already sense in your gut: The first meeting is pivotal to increasing win rates. The first meeting is the deal foundation and lays the groundwork for an energized deal. When it's weak, the deal teeters, often crumbling before it can gain traction.

Unfortunately, few companies have a clearly defined, repeatable strategy for handling first meetings. Instead, they assume the salespeople they hire already know how to navigate this critical step effectively. That assumption, as you may have experienced firsthand, is deeply flawed.

This issue—this glaring omission—is why I wrote *The First Meeting Differentiator*.

Sales organizations underperform because they leave this critical aspect of the sales process to chance. And this isn't a modern problem. Everything I've said so far was as true a century ago as it is today, and it will remain true for generations to come. Why? Because the principles of human connection, trust building, and differentiation are timeless.

Whether your first meeting lasts fifteen minutes or two hours, there are nonnegotiable elements that must be addressed. You need to qualify the deal, differentiate what and how you sell, and create emotional engagement. The specifics will vary depending on your industry and the complexity of your sale, but the underlying objectives remain constant.

While many sales books touch on the importance of the first meeting and sprinkle in a few tips or strategies, none dedicate themselves to the topic comprehensively. A structured, step-by-step guide to mastering the first meeting didn't exist—until now.

For more than thirty-five years, I've worked with sales organizations to craft first meeting strategies that have led to record-breaking results. Whether I led sales teams directly or consulted with clients, I saw first-hand how a thoughtful, intentional approach to the first meeting could transform win rates and protect margins. You'll find this book is written as a workbook, designed to equip you with everything you need to build a rock-solid first meeting framework based on proven, real-world strategies.

This book is for both sales management executives and individual revenue contributors. For sales managers, it provides a blueprint for creating a scalable, repeatable first meeting strategy across your organization. For salespeople, it offers actionable guidance to elevate your individual performance. The strategy presented here applies to B2B and complex B2C sales, whether you're selling products, services, technology, or SaaS solutions.

You may have noticed that I refer to the "first meeting" rather than "discovery." There's a reason for that, which I'll explain in chapter 1. Suffice it to say for now that the first meeting is so much more than simply uncovering needs; it's about setting the tone for the entire relationship. It's about showing your buyer that you understand them, that you're different from everyone else vying for their attention, and that you're uniquely equipped to help them succeed.

So, why should you read this book? Because it will empower you with the strategy, tactics, and tools to consistently win deals—and do so without slashing your margins. Winning isn't just about selling more; it's about selling smart.

I'll leave you with this thought: If you want to *win more deals at the prices you want*®, you need a better first meeting strategy. It's as simple as that. And this book will teach you how to craft and execute that strategy.

Are you ready to elevate your sales game? Let's start the journey together.

CHAPTER 1

THE NECESSARY DEATH
OF DISCOVERY MEETINGS

I f you are familiar with my work, you know I'm a sales contrarian. I oppose the commonplace sales strategies, tactics, and tools preached to salespeople. These strategies, though frequently used, are ineffective. Some are outdated, while others never worked in the first place. Salespeople need real-world, proven strategies and tactics that help them *win more deals at the prices you want®*, and that starts with how to approach the first meeting.

Traditional discovery meetings must die. The time has come to put those meetings that solely focus on a salesperson's needs out of their misery. You may ask, Why? Discovery meetings don't make salespeople miserable. True! The misery belongs to the prospective clients forced to sit through these painful, one-sided meetings.

I'm on a mission to eradicate the sales mindset taught to salespeople since the beginning of sales time, which says, "The first meeting is a discovery meeting."

Discovery Meetings: A Relic of the Past

For my clients reading this, you are probably curious about my perspective on the first meeting, given that I've worked with you and your sales teams to develop your discovery strategies. Yes, I have used the word *discovery*. As a student of sales, however, I've come to realize the term is problematic. The reason is that discovery meetings have one primary beneficiary: the salesperson. The public knows that when they hear the word *discovery* from a salesperson, the sole purpose of that interaction is to benefit the salesperson.

Picture this: After months of prospecting into an account, you finally secure a first meeting with a Decision Influencer (Decision Influencers, or DIs, affect the decision to buy what you sell). Excited, you dive in with the classic agenda-setting strategy that has been taught to salespeople since the beginning of sales time as a best practice:

> **What I want to do today is ask you some questions about your business and then tell you about what we offer.**

Do you see a problem? Those two words—"I want"—convey that the meeting is entirely for the salesperson's benefit and imply that the salesperson doesn't care whether the DI derives any meaningful value from it. Right in the first few moments, the salesperson has blown the meeting because of the message they conveyed. It's no wonder that so many studies reveal that DIs are frustrated with their first meeting experience with salespeople.

Here's a sales fact: No one cares what you want—except, perhaps, your mother. Decision Influencers are busy. They're skeptical. Many have been burned by salespeople. When you make the first meeting all about yourself, you validate their worst fears. How can you possibly build a relationship during the first meeting when you've made the DI feel this way? You can't!

People aren't wrong about perceiving the first meeting as exclusively for the salesperson's benefit, are they? Nowhere does that agenda-setting message say that the DI will gain any benefit from the time spent with you. Do you know why it isn't mentioned? Because a discovery meeting mindset places all the emphasis on the salesperson's needs, wants, and desires.

This perspective is not theoretical. It's a painful sales reality. I challenge salespeople on this point when I ask them,

> **What value do Decision Influencers receive from a first meeting with you?**

The most common response is a puzzled look followed by an uncomfortable silence. Why? Because most salespeople have not even considered the first meeting from that perspective. Salespeople are so focused on getting what *they* want from the meeting that they fail to give even the slightest thought to the value the other person might receive.

We all know that prospecting is tough. Reaching someone on the phone or receiving a response to an email is challenging. When you are finally lucky enough to connect with a DI live, more often than not, they decline to take a meeting with you. The reason is that the sales industry has created the impression that these meetings are a waste of time for the DI; they provide no value to them, just for the salesperson. Given that perception, why would anyone agree to meet with a salesperson?

It's also not uncommon to see an email signature or a call to action on a website that states, "Schedule a Discovery Meeting." The implication is, "You are about to sit through a sales call." No one wants to sign up for that experience because they know its sole purpose is for the salesperson to acquire information to sell them something and it will not be time well invested for the DI. We may as well have a sign offering free root canals. People would be just as excited by that message.

I'm not suggesting that the first meeting should not include discovery elements. For example, "deal qualifying" absolutely needs to be a component: Determining if this is the right deal to pursue is essential. But it can't be the meeting's sole purpose. We need to change our sales mindset. Salespeople can no longer look at the first meeting solely through the lens of discovery. They need a broader perspective.

The Case for Consultations

Now, let's flip the script. Imagine if, instead of a discovery meeting, your first interaction was a consultation. Think about when you have had an illness or an injury and scheduled a meeting with a doctor. Why did you go to the doctor? For two primary reasons: to become wiser about your issue and to understand potential remedies. You undoubtedly didn't expect to feel like the interaction was entirely for the doctor's benefit or you were part of a research study. Yet that's how most Decision Influencers feel during the first meeting: It is just for the salesperson's benefit. Doctors don't refer to that interaction as a discovery meeting. They refer to it as a *consultation*.

Decision Influencers despise discovery experiences because they don't receive meaningful value from them. On the other hand, they greatly appreciate well-facilitated consultations. The first meeting can't just be about a salesperson gathering information; it must also include delivering meaningful value to the DI. Just as with the medical scenario, if someone agrees to a consultation with you, they expect to become wiser about their issues and to understand potential remedies. You must achieve both during your consultations for the deal to advance.

Changing the name of the first meeting isn't wordplay. It's a mindset shift, a strategic selling decision. I challenge you to look up the word *consultation* in the dictionary or thesaurus. Neither the definition nor the synonyms bear any resemblance to the way most salespeople conduct their first meeting. According to Dictionary.com, a consultation is a meeting for deliberation and discussion. From that same source, discovery is the act or process of seeing, finding, or gaining knowledge of something previously unknown. Discovery meetings, then, are primarily fact-finding expeditions for salespeople rather than the deliberations and discussions DIs desire.

Imagine perceiving your first meeting with a DI as a consultation rather than a discovery. Immediately, your mindset changes. What you believe, you become. That's the power of the mind.

If you believe you are conducting consultations rather than discovery meetings, your first meeting strategy changes and differentiates you.

You recognize that the first meeting can't just be solely for your benefit. The person you are meeting with must also receive meaningful value— that is, if you want to have subsequent meetings moving toward consummating a deal. The first step to changing the perception of the first meeting is to change your agenda-setting approach. Rather than making a statement, ask a question to collaborate on the agenda:

> **For this to be a great use of your time, what do you want to make sure we talk about today?**

Their answer provides two important benefits to you. First, they have just told you what is most important to them, which allows you to focus on those aspects. Second, right at the beginning of the first meeting, you've communicated that you genuinely care that they find the interaction meaningful.

What Is Meaningful Value?

So how do you know if they received meaningful value from the first meeting? Without your prompting, they say something at the end of the meeting like this:

> **I'm so glad we met. This meeting was a great use of my time.**

I'm sure you have occasionally heard that from DIs. At least, I hope you have. But what if receiving that feedback becomes one of the Desired Consultation Outcomes you seek? If you achieve that, you've succeeded in changing the perception of the first meeting, setting the stage for future productive interactions with them. If they haven't made that statement, I like to ask: "So, how did we do today?" with an expectation of a positive response regarding the time spent together.

The first step to consistently achieving that Outcome is to shift your mindset from perceiving that interaction as a one-dimensional discovery session to a mutually meaningful consultation. With this mindset, you will always think about the answer to the following question:

> **What does the DI get out of the first meeting?**

This mindset shift will also help you set more meetings during prospecting. And what salesperson doesn't want that? As I mentioned earlier, people have been conditioned to believe that the sole purpose of the first meeting is for the salesperson's benefit. Once you have determined what meaningful value DIs can receive from a first meeting with you, include that messaging in your outreach. If you do, you'll differentiate yourself from the hundreds of salespeople trying to get their attention. Most of them will never get to have a live conversation with that DI. But you will have a much better chance because you conveyed to the DI that they will receive something meaningful during the first meeting.

You are now probably wondering about the meaningful value DIs could derive from you during a consultation. Consider this:

> **Who knows more about the world of potential solutions in your industry: you or the people you sell to?**

I've asked that question of salespeople in every industry, in companies of all sizes, and in countries all around the world. Every time, I receive the same answer: "*Me!*" Not once has a salesperson said that the people they sell to know more than they do about the world of potential solutions in their industry. Given that, here's my question for you to ponder:

> **What do you know, that DIs don't know, but need to know now?**

The answer to that question helps you identify the potential meaningful value you can offer. It is important to note that meaningful value cannot just be the features and benefits of what you sell: "They'll learn about what we offer." That's not the meaningful value DIs want from a first meeting. They should derive meaningful value during the consultation regardless of what you sell.

Here are some examples of your opportunities to provide meaningful value. Select only ones that DIs are likely unaware of and related to what you sell.

- A best practice in your industry that could help them.
- A new trend in your or their industry that they need to be aware of.
- A study that can help them in their role.
- A way to identify areas of inefficiency.

- A new regulation that may affect them.
- An opportunity to reduce cost.
- What their competitors are doing that they are missing out on.
- A way for them to increase revenue or acquire clients.
- An opportunity for them to differentiate themselves from the competition.
- An update on common compliance issues and how to avoid them.

I bet as you read that list, the wheels started turning for you. Great! Make that first meeting mindset shift now from discovery to consultation. There's no reason not to immediately implement the concept of "providing DIs with meaningful value" during the first meeting. It's game-changing! If they receive meaningful value from you, they are more likely to have future interactions with you.

Some changes take a while to see results. Not this one. You will experience a difference immediately because DIs will have a different first meeting experience with you. And providing meaningful value doesn't happen just during the consultation. I challenge you to look at every sales interaction as an opportunity to provide meaningful value to your DIs.

Also, once you identify your meaningful value, you can take the next step to elevate your consultation agenda approach.

> Thank you for investing time with me today. My recommendation is we start with an overview of your business. Then I will share with you some trends we see in your industry. Once we talk through those, we can discuss what my company offers. For this to be a great use of your time, what else do you want to make sure we talk about today?

Notice the use of the word *investing* in the first sentence. You want the DI to know that you recognize and appreciate that they agreed to this meeting instead of working on the twenty tasks on their plate. They are making a time investment in a potential relationship with you.

The next sentence also has an important word in it: *recommendation*. Earlier in the chapter, I reminded you that you have a level of expertise in your arena that your DIs do not. They want and need you to lead them on this journey. They will usually positively accept your recommendation on how to start the meeting because within that recommendation, you mentioned the meaningful value they will receive and opened the door for them to share what they wanted to accomplish with you.

The Deal Foundation

Taking a step back, why is this consultation mindset shift so significant to your success? The first meeting is the foundation of the deal. If the consultation is weak, the deal is weak. When a building has a weak foundation, what happens? The structure crumbles. The same happens to deals when first meetings are mishandled. If you want to increase your win rate, stop worrying about developing manipulative closing techniques and focus on improving how you handle the first meeting: *the consultation*.

We all know that sales is a game of inches. One word, a phrase, or a question can be the difference between winning or losing. It has also become harder and harder to differentiate what you sell. Couple that with how busy executives are and how incredibly challenging it is to get DIs to accept a meeting. How salespeople handle the first meeting is vital to their success in winning deals.

You may have wondered why this chapter emphasized the beginning of the consultation: the consultation agenda. Given that the first meeting is the deal foundation, the start sets the tone for the DI's overall experience with you. You would be amazed how many first meetings were over before they began because of how the salesperson started the meeting.

When you book the first meeting, the consultation mindset helps you meaningfully differentiate yourself in ways the competition has not. Note the repeated use of the word *meaningful* in this chapter. Different for the sake of different fails to provide value during the interaction. The difference must be of value to the DI, which is why I inserted the word *meaningfully* before the word *differentiate*.

First Meeting Preparation

Coming back to the medical consultation example, several steps occurred before you met with the doctor. The receptionist asked for your health insurance information and handed you a form to complete that captured your background health information. When it was your turn to be seen, a nurse walked you to the examination room and took your vitals. They also reviewed your medical history and asked about your current ailment. They documented all this information and provided it to the doctor in preparation for a masterful consultation.

The parallel to sales is in how you plan and prepare for your consultation, which is such an important topic that I've dedicated chapter 4 to it.

While the health background information you provided is critical to the consultation's success, that alone is not enough for the doctor to fully understand the issue, explain it to you, and discuss potential remedies. The doctor's preparation began many years earlier when they attended medical school. They took years of classes in various sciences, observed medical professionals in action, participated in a residency program, and even learned how to conduct effective consultations.

Even after they graduated from medical school and became a licensed doctor, their learning was not over. New advancements are continually discussed, debated, and introduced into the medical profession, so doctors must be insatiable in their quest to learn and keep their knowledge and skills current.

Interestingly, the medical profession prohibits students from seeing patients independently. They are permitted to do so only once they have demonstrated medical mastery and become a licensed doctor. I wish the sales world required a demonstration of mastery before salespeople could sell independently. That would certainly move the sales needle and change the common negative perception DIs have of salespeople.

Given the number of times you have gone for medical consultations, I bet you can't name a single time when you felt your doctor was winging it. I'll take it a step further. You likely never felt the doctor was making up information and telling you what you wanted to hear. Good luck trying to push a doctor to provide a diagnosis and remedy before they are prepared to do so. It won't happen. Medical professionals are obligated to their patients to thoroughly complete their analysis before providing diagnoses and recommendations. Unfortunately, we can't say the same of most salespeople. They commonly share diagnoses and recommendations without fully understanding the circumstances and are not well versed in the appropriate solutions. Sometimes, salespeople even allow prospective clients to muscle them into providing a diagnosis (a solution) without completing their analysis. If you embrace the consultation mindset, you won't allow that to happen because you won't be forced into a solution diagnosis prematurely. You'll lead a discussion by taking DIs down an understandable path, so they recognize when the appropriate time has come to discuss a solution.

The Title No One Can Give You

The sales industry is chock-full of titles employers give to salespeople. But there is one title that no one can give you: sales professional. You must earn it. No one can make you a sales professional. You must take the necessary steps to develop that mastery.

When a workplace drug testing company hired me as vice president of marketing and sales, I didn't know the first thing about the product or the industry. My prior two roles were sales management positions in technology. But I recognized that to succeed, I needed to master the industry and the solutions we offered. More specifically, I needed to become an expert in the topics that Decision Influencers care about so I could provide meaningful value when interacting with them. To conduct consultations successfully, I needed to know more than they did about the issues that mattered most to them.

So I immersed myself in the space. Within months, I had gained more expertise in workplace drug testing than anyone else on my sales team, many of whom had been in the industry for more than a decade. People often confuse experience with expertise. Just because you've spent time in an industry (experience) doesn't mean you've mastered it (expertise).

When I traveled with my salespeople to prospect and client meetings, the depth of my knowledge shocked my team because they knew I was not hired from within the industry. After these *joint* (I had to use the word given that this was the workplace drug testing industry) meetings, my salespeople began receiving tremendously positive feedback from Decision Influencers. This was due to the meaningful value we provided by sharing industry trends, competitor strategies, and ways to protect their businesses. In fact, the Decision Influencers often thought I was an industry consultant due to my in-depth knowledge of topics that mattered to them, which indicated they had experienced a meaningful *consultation*.

I didn't share this story to pat myself on the back. I included it to explain that I didn't do anything my salespeople couldn't have—but hadn't—done themselves. I recognized that this mastery was critical to my success, especially when conducting consultations. And I invested a ton of time learning.

Top salespeople have a passion for continuous learning. They don't feel like it's a menial task but rather that it's a critical aspect of their success and their ability to conduct meaningful (there's that word again) consultations.

This industry-immersion exercise wasn't a one-time deal for me. Each time I started in a new industry, I took the same immersion approach to master what was most important to Decision Influencers so I could conduct meaningful consultations, an approach that worked every time.

Salespeople, while I encourage you to change your mindset of the first meeting from a discovery to a consultation, know that you can't masterfully conduct a consultation until you have developed a high enough level of expertise in your arena to deliver meaningful value to the DI. Don't wait for your sales manager to tap you on the shoulder and tell you to do it. That shoulder tap results from them observing you failing to provide meaningful value during the meetings, which means those meetings failed to be consultations. If you want to be considered a sales professional, recognize the importance of developing this mastery and do something about it every single day. Read a book (you can check the box for that one today). Watch a video. Conduct research. I share this with my clients:

> **Do something today and every day to make yourself more valuable to your prospects and clients tomorrow.**

The patient could die if a doctor, out of negligence, makes a misdiagnosis during a consultation. Salespeople who are negligent in handling consultations can kill their deals.

But how do you create an effective consultation framework? You start by selecting Desired Consultation Outcomes, which you'll learn about in chapter 2.

THE FIRST MEETING DIFFERENTIATOR: CONCEPT #1

The first meeting should be perceived not as a discovery but as a consultation to ensure the person you meet with also receives meaningful value from the interaction. The consultation is the foundation of the deal. If the consultation is weak, the deal is weak and likely to collapse.

WHAT COMPRISES A SUCCESSFUL FIRST MEETING?

Years ago, I served as the chief sales officer for a multitier sales organization. We had a team of eight regional vice presidents (RVPs), each with five sales representatives on their teams. One sales representative was asked to deliver a presentation about our capabilities (not a consultation meeting) to a significant manufacturing prospect in Chicago. On the sales representative's behalf, the RVP asked me to join the meeting and present an overview of our company, which I, of course, agreed to do.

I flew into O'Hare on the day of the meeting and met the RVP and sales representative at a coffee shop a few hours before the meeting. After some fun Cubs conversation, I turned the discussion to business and asked what I thought was an innocuous question:

> We know we are not going to leave this meeting with a deal. It will be a great meeting if we accomplish what?

The two of them looked at me as if I had sixteen heads and stared at me in silence. They had no idea what I was asking. We started talking, and I explained the context for the question: What would make this meeting a success? While they had spent a lot of time assembling a random list of questions to ask and message points to share, they had not even considered the goals they wanted to achieve. My "innocuous question" quickly developed into a deep conversation about the meeting strategy, and we completely retooled our approach.

As I flew back to Minneapolis, I kept thinking about the coffee shop question I asked. How could salespeople appropriately prepare for a sales interaction without defining the success criteria? So I started asking my "great meeting question criteria" of other salespeople on my team. I received the same reaction from each of them as I had at the coffee shop. That was a head-scratcher. I came back to my question as I flew home:

> **How can salespeople develop a sales interaction game plan if they haven't first defined what would make it a success?**

I hosted a meeting of our RVPs to talk about this issue and presented a consultation strategy they could implement with their salespeople. This strategy is what I refer to as "reverse engineering the consultation." While this book focuses on the first meeting, this strategy I present applies to all sales interactions.

Before the team learned this strategy, they would prepare for a sales interaction by developing a list of questions and message points. The flaw with that approach is that while you can ask an infinite number of questions, the DI will tolerate only so many. And the questions you do ask may not be the right ones. Many salespeople can talk about their company and what they offer for sixteen hours, but no DI will grant them a meeting of that duration, nor is it necessary.

Obviously, that approach didn't work.

Effectively developing a consultation strategy necessitates starting with identifying the Outcomes that would make for a great consultation. Then, and only then, can you determine the right questions, message points, and actions.

In the bestselling book *The 7 Habits of Highly Effective People*, Stephen R. Covey shared similar advice when he asserted that the second habit is to "Begin with the end in mind."

The Troublesome Perspective Question

Over the years, I've had several opportunities to pose one of my favorite questions to executives:

If all your salespeople called you and said they just had a great consultation, what would you know, for certain, took place during that meeting?

The most common answer is an uncomfortable look and an awkward silence. Why? Because they have never defined their company's consultation strategy. While they all agree that the consultation is the deal foundation, as a leadership team, they haven't prescribed how to properly handle this critical step.

I asked a similar question of salespeople, particularly those within the same sales organization, selling the same products and services to the same market segment:

What are your criteria for a great consultation?

After a brief pause, each salesperson shared their perspective, and each one had a different answer. How can that be? They are selling the same stuff to the same people in the same market segment, but they perceived my question as an opinion question. A prerequisite to sales organization success is that everyone answers this question the same way.

Bridging the gap between what the executive views as a successful first meeting and what the salesperson considers a good first meeting paints the picture of the issue. Executives have not prescribed the process for developing a consultation strategy, which forces their salespeople to develop their own approach. The absence of a prescribed consultation strategy leads to four major issues:

1. Best practices are not leveraged.
2. Mistakes are made repeatedly.
3. Differentiation is inconsistent.
4. Troubleshooting is nearly impossible because every salesperson has their own way of approaching the consultation.

Taking it a step further, here's a scary fact about companies that fail to prescribe their sales process: The less defined the steps are, the greater the likelihood salespeople will fail or underperform.

I have developed what I call a Sales Organization Environment Spectrum. At one end is an "Entrepreneurial" environment; on the other, an "Execution" environment. In most instances, Entrepreneurial is perceived as a positive, but not in this context. An Entrepreneurial sales environment is one where salespeople bear the burden of developing the sales strategy entirely on their own. As a result, failure and underperformance are unacceptably high because many salespeople lack the skill set to create their own sales environment. This in turn leads to inconsistent and erratic results as well as high turnover.

At the other end of the spectrum, sales organizations that have Execution environments have fully defined processes. Think in terms of manufacturing a product. Manufacturers teach their teams how the work is to be done, how the product is to be assembled, and how their processes are to be executed. As a result of being process-based, they are scalable with predictable, consistent results.

The same holds true for sales organizations. The more defined the processes, the more scalable and consistent the sales performance. If you read that and think I'm an advocate for creating sales robots, you are mistaken. Salespeople need a framework of defined processes that allow them plenty of opportunity for personalization, which is also essential to their success.

The first meeting strategy is a significant component of that sales system, which many sales organizations leave to their salespeople to determine. As mentioned, that is a flawed approach. We are going to resolve this issue right here, right now, starting with this foundational question about developing a consultation strategy:

It was a great consultation if what was accomplished?

As this question implies, the starting point for developing a consultation strategy begins with defining what makes the first meeting a success. Imagine the meeting is over, and you are walking back to your car or ending a virtual meeting. What Outcomes will have made the meeting a success? In other words, the first step in developing a consultation strategy is to define the Outcomes that would make for a great consultation. Only once you have identified those can you determine what questions to ask and what message points to convey because they are a function of the Desired Consultation Outcomes.

Notice the use of the word *great* to describe the consultation. Our goal should always be to have great consultations. And that's exactly what this strategy aims to help you accomplish.

Unless you expect to walk out of a first meeting with a signed deal, this consultation development strategy has one overarching objective:

Pique a high enough level of interest with Decision Influencers that they want to continue interacting with you after the consultation.

If you embrace that objective, your entire approach to consultation strategy development changes. Rather than being concerned about asking every possible question and telling the DI about everything you offer, you become much more selective. If you spark enough curiosity during the consultation, there will be more interactions, which means you can ask some questions and share some information at another time.

The converse is also true. If you don't ask the right questions or don't share information compellingly, you may not get another opportunity to interact with them.

Trying to accomplish too much during the consultation is flawed. Accomplishing too little is also flawed. The key is accomplishing the right set of Desired Consultation Outcomes to keep the deal moving forward.

It is also important to note that the set of Desired Consultation Outcomes will vary depending upon with whom you are meeting. Let's say you sell copiers and have one consultation each with a CFO, a marketing manager, and an IT manager. The Desired Consultation Outcomes and, thus, the first meeting with each of them must be different. Why? Because the information they can share with you, what will pique their interest, and what will motivate them to have further interactions with you varies based on their role. A consultation strategy is needed for every Decision Influencer with whom you will have consultations.

Determining the Consultation Foundation

I'm about to share some potential Desired Consultation Outcomes to consider for your list. But before I do, I want to challenge you to think about this question for each Outcome:

> **Do I need to accomplish this Outcome during the consultation or can it happen during another part of the sales process?**

That question brings you back to my point about the consultation's overarching objective: to pique enough interest with the DI that they want to continue conversations with you after the consultation. As you will see, there are a ton of potential Outcomes that could be achieved during the consultation. The question is which ones must you accomplish to achieve the overarching objective of having future interactions. As I mentioned, you want to achieve just the right set of Desired Consultation Outcomes.

The first part of identifying the Outcomes that make up a great consultation is to focus on what information you need to acquire. A primary reason for obtaining that information is to qualify the deal. This topic is so important that I've dedicated the entire next chapter to it.

When selecting Desired Consultation Outcomes, the first question to ask yourself is:

What information must I learn during the consultation?

Note the underlined expression "must I learn," which refers to my earlier point that you don't need to ask every question during the first meeting. Rather, you need to carefully consider which information you must learn during the consultation and which you can learn later.

■

THE CONSULTATION FOUNDATION WORKSHOP

To help you with what you are about to read, download my Consultation Outcomes worksheet at **www.ConsultationOutcomes .com**. This tool will help you quickly implement this component of the first meeting differentiator strategy.

Depending on whether this opportunity came from an inbound lead or an outbound-generated opportunity, the following Desired Consultation Outcomes may be on your list to achieve.

■ **How they heard about you.** This is helpful to know to gauge marketing campaign effectiveness. The better the marketing team knows what is working (and not), the better they can assist with lead generation.

Alternatively, the lead could have come to you through a referral source or be a former user/client, which again makes this Outcome essential to achieve.

In most cases, however, you should achieve this Outcome before the consultation, particularly when you schedule it. If that conversation did not take place, then it belongs on your Desired Consultation Outcomes list.

■ **Why they contacted you.** The reason they contacted you is never your marketing or advertising campaign. There is a deeper reason that must be uncovered. The ad may have been the impetus, but the reason for contacting you is much more than that. Something is happening in the organization, and the ad was merely the trigger to investigate a resolution.

Just like the prior Outcome, you should achieve this before the consultation, preferably when you scheduled the meeting. But if that conversation did not occur, learning this information belongs on your Desired Consultation Outcomes list.

■ **Why they accepted the meeting.** This is particularly relevant when you booked a consultation because of your prospecting. If you aren't 100 percent certain about the reason the DI agreed to meet with you, then you should learn that answer during the consultation. Also, achieving this Outcome early in the consultation will help guide you on what is most important to discuss during the meeting and can chart the course for it.

Information Acquisition

The following section delves into information acquisition, which I've organized into three sections: Current Circumstance, Future Solution, and Decision Framework. I've provided an explanation of each potential Outcome to help you implement the strategy. Readers of this book range from non-salespeople to those new to sales to skilled veterans. These summaries ensure you can implement this strategy component regardless of your prior knowledge and skill level.

Current Circumstance

Current Circumstance is intended to develop a comprehensive understanding of their present situation. Outcomes include: the current situation, how it is being provided, who is providing it, and the satisfaction level with how it is being provided.

You'll notice that the expression "current situation" is used rather than "current solution." By definition, a solution means the problem is being solved. Referring to their current situation as a "solution" unintentionally validates it, which is not great positioning given that your goal is to displace the incumbent.

- **What the current situation is, how it is being provided, and by whom.** Knowing this information helps you select relevant differentiators to share during the consultation. Without learning this, you may share information that makes you sound the same as what they currently have and are potentially seeking to replace.

- **The level of satisfaction with the current situation and why.** Understanding the DI's level of satisfaction is important, but it is not enough of a Desired Outcome on its own. You also need to understand why the DI is unsatisfied because that can expose positioning opportunities for what you offer.

- **What they have done in the past (and are currently doing) to address their dissatisfaction and the results of those efforts.** Knowing this information will allow you to avoid making suggestions and recommendations that the DI has already tried and that have already failed to achieve the desired results.

- **Who is impacted by the issues, how, and why.** For the solutions you recommend to be valid and targeted to their issues, you need to develop a complete picture of their Current Circumstances. If you don't understand who the issues impact, how they affect them, and why, you risk the DI not embracing your solution. Many issues can be described in financial terms. If the financial impact can be quantified, and if it's a substantial number, their interest in pursuing a resolution will likely skyrocket.

- **The renewal/termination provisions in the current provider's contract.** In some industries, the contract renewal/termination language is onerous and makes it difficult for their clients to cancel. If you are targeting one of those industries, you would want to know this information because it could affect your overall account-selling strategy.

- **What they are paying for the current situation.** Learning this information is essential because it exposes potential financial alignment issues/opportunities between what they are paying today versus what an investment in your solution would be. If they are paying significantly less for their current situation, there is a conversation to be had to determine if they are willing to make a greater investment for a superior solution.

- **The payment terms with their current provider.** This also exposes potential financial alignment issues/opportunities. The current provider may offer more stringent or liberal terms than you offer, which could be seen as a positive differentiator or an issue requiring careful navigation.

Future Solution

Future Solution is intended to develop a comprehensive understanding of their intended direction for the relationship. Outcomes include: objectives, scope, requirements, and competition.

- **The scope of the opportunity.** This is your understanding of the magnitude, complexities, and needs of this opportunity. It's developing a complete picture of what a new solution with your company would look like. You may also find that this opportunity is not a good fit for your company.

- **What they know about and their perspective of your company.** Knowing this helps you select the appropriate information to share. Your approach with someone deeply familiar with your company will vastly differ from the one you take with someone who knows little. This Outcome also goes deeper than the facts they know. It delves into how they perceive your company. In most cases, they wouldn't be meeting with you if their perceptions were negative. But they may, for example, be concerned that you are too big (or small) to manage their account properly.

- **Others they are considering and why.** This is tricky. They may not be talking with any other providers, and if you ask directly about it, that could plant the seed that they should be shopping their business. It could create unnecessary competition. But if you ask indirect questions about their situation and their ideas to resolve their issues, you may discover if they are also talking with your competitors.

- **Their perspective of options provided by others under consideration.** If you have determined that they are exploring a relationship with other players in your space, it's important to understand what they like and don't like about what they've seen from those providers.

- **Their perspective regarding the right solution for their objectives.** Most DIs have a perspective about the solution they need. It may or may not be correct or comprehensive, but learning what they are thinking is essential.

- **The alignment between their needs and what you offer.** How do their requirements align with what your company provides? A lack of alignment should tell you this deal is not likely to come to fruition.

- **Their organization's readiness for and acceptance of a solution change.** Change is scary, and most people are not excited about it. Every organization has a different tolerance for change relative to the issues they are experiencing and what they are trying to accomplish. Knowing who within their organization will support and who will rebuff change is important for both you and the DI to understand. This Outcome could also affect your client onboarding strategy to give them the confidence they need to say yes to your solution.

- **The company's level of desire and urgency to make a change and why.** As I share in chapter 6 about pain, people will vent and complain but may not be prepared to address the issues they are experiencing. It could be because the situation isn't bad enough to take on the work associated with change, or perhaps the organization has a general resistance to change. Regardless of the reason, if their desire and sense of urgency to make the change isn't sufficient to overcome those organizational hurdles, you need to either help them recognize that they need to address the issue(s) or you should stop pursuing the deal because it's likely not going to happen.

Decision Framework

Decision Framework is intended to develop a comprehensive understanding of how DIs will make their decision. Outcomes include: the decision-making group, decision-making process, as well as price and contract considerations.

- **Their requirements for making a change.** This can be very telling and will expose the alignment (or lack thereof) between your company and what you offer relative to their priorities.

- **The Decision Influencers involved with evaluating the solution.** At some point, you want to find out who will be involved in the decision-making process. The question is whether you need to determine "the who" during the first meeting.

- **Their level of influence in the decision-making process.** It is essential to determine the decision-making influence of the DI you are meeting with during the consultation. Again, the question to consider is, when does this need to be accomplished?

- **The process they will use to determine the viability of a new solution.** Understanding how they will evaluate proposed solutions will help you determine how to prepare an overall deal-pursuit strategy.

- **The decision-making process.** Understanding the decision-making journey and how they will choose a solution will also allow you to prepare an overall deal-pursuit strategy. It can also expose whether they require a formal buying process, such as a request for proposal (RFP).

- **The priority of this initiative relative to other initiatives and why.** You may have noticed a reoccurring theme of "why." Knowing the priority of this initiative is important, but if you don't also know why, you risk having alignment issues with your created solution.

- **Their timeline to make a decision and why.** This information can be very telling, especially whether their response is vague or specific. If they are unclear about the timeline, they may not have a high level of decision-making authority for this deal, or the issue may not be important enough for them to address quickly. If they are specific, there will likely be momentum toward making a change.

■ **Their timeline to have a new solution implemented and why.** For the same reasons as the prior Outcome, this one is essential to achieve. Like the other Outcomes, the question for you to answer is when you need to achieve it.

■ **What needs to happen for their timeline to be met and what potential obstacles may be encountered.** When DIs share timelines, salespeople sometimes become euphoric and feel that a deal is imminent. Understanding what could stand in the way of achieving the timeline is essential. This information isn't important just for the salesperson, but it also helps the DI think through potential hurdles and barriers.

■ **The funding source for this initiative.** Usually, DIs meet with salespeople because they have an issue they need to address. Unfortunately, they sometimes fail to identify where the dollars will come from to pay for what they are interested in buying. If they don't have (and are not likely to get) the dollars, pursuing the opportunity can be a waste of your time. When DIs don't know how they will fund the solution, that should raise a significant concern for the salesperson.

■ **Their current corporate goals/future corporate strategy initiatives and how you fit within them.** Most deals are in jeopardy if the solution does not align with current and future company goals. This lack of alignment can make it challenging to get the time, dollars, and resources needed for a deal to come together.

■ **Their personal goals and how you fit within them.** Executives have more than enough on their plates. Initiatives

not tied to their individual (and/or corporate) goals will likely
fizzle out due to other priorities taking precedence.

- **The business drivers associated with the identified
  objectives and issues.** This Outcome is your (and their)
  understanding of the financial justification to buy what you sell.
  Examples of business drivers include: cost reduction, revenue
  growth, and profitability increase.

All of the prior Outcomes result from questions asked of a DI and
paying careful attention to verbal and nonverbal responses. Often-
times, one question can potentially accomplish multiple Outcomes,
which is a reminder not to select too many or too few Outcomes for
your consultation list. Remember the overarching objective of the
consultation: *to spark a high enough level of interest with the DI so
there will be future interactions.*

In addition to gathering information, other *Outcomes* need to be
achieved. The next section of *Outcomes* may necessitate questions being asked, information being shared visually or verbally, and/
or actions being taken before, during, or after the consultation to
achieve them. As you read through them, challenge yourself to select
only the ones that must be accomplished during the consultation.

Additional Outcomes That MUST Be Achieved

The following Outcomes must be achieved for any sale type. The
question is when and how to achieve the Outcome. Some of these
can be achieved through pre-consultation research while others can
be achieved during the consultation or at some other time.

- **Shared relevant company background information.** In
  the Future Solution section, one Outcome concerned your
  understanding of what they know about your company and
  their perspectives of it. If you selected that Outcome, this

one is also necessary. The key is sharing relevant information based on what the DI already knows.

- **Shared relevant product/solution information.** Related to the prior Outcome, this one is sharing pertinent information about what you offer, the solution. The level of detail you share is a function of the type of consultation you conduct. You may have a high-level discussion regarding your capabilities or get specific and design a detailed solution for them.

- **Positioned relevant differentiators, and those differentiators matter to the DI(s).** This Outcome has two parts. Certainly check the box that you shared your differentiators. But this Outcome isn't just about sharing information. It is about creating excitement with the DI regarding your differentiators. If they aren't excited about your differentiators, prepare for an uncomfortable price discussion when you present a proposal. Thus the use of the word *relevant*. Select the right differentiators that will resonate with this DI under these circumstances.

- **Set defined action steps with a timeline.** If the consultation has gone well, salespeople should conclude the meeting by defining the next steps with a corresponding timeline. That approach communicates a high level of sales professionalism and keeps the deal moving forward.

- **Scheduled a follow-up meeting.** Similar to the prior Outcome, this is also a super important one to achieve, and salespeople don't commit to this one often enough. Whenever you interact with a DI, there should always be a scheduled next interaction with them.

- **Gained interest in exploring a relationship with your company.** This Outcome gets to the consultation's core objective, which is to pique a high enough level of interest that the DI wants to have future interactions with you. Unless you are completing a sale during the consultation and no further connection is desired with the DI after the sale, this one is key to achieve.

- **Established trust and took the first steps toward building a relationship.** This is another must-have unless you are consummating sales during the consultation and you desire no further connection with the DI after the sale. Without trust, you cannot achieve the prior Outcome of gaining the DI's interest in exploring a relationship with your company.

- **Gave them confidence in our ability to handle their account.** Buyer skepticism and fear of change are significant Deal Obstacles salespeople encounter during deal pursuits. Ensuring the DI has confidence in your company's ability to support their account properly will help overcome those obstacles.

- **Differentiated yourself and provided meaningful value.** In my books *Sales Differentiation* and *Sell Different!*, I share the importance of salespeople differentiating themselves by delivering meaningful value when selling. Differentiation started during prospecting and continues during and past the first meeting.

- **Transitioned their emotions.** People buy based on emotions and justify their decisions with logic. If the consultation does not arouse their emotions, there is a high risk of the deal fizzling out. In chapter 5, you will learn how to develop Empathetic Expertise to facilitate emotional transitions.

- **Showed appreciation for them meeting with you.** This Outcome may appear basic and elementary, but it is vital. No executive has ever been hired with the sole responsibility of meeting with salespeople on an hourly basis. They are super busy! That they invested their time to meet with you deserves demonstrable appreciation. Simply thanking them for investing time with you can help achieve this Outcome. Too few salespeople do this.

- **They thought the meeting was a great use of their time.** As covered in chapter 1, a common mistake is for the salesperson to perceive the first meeting as a discovery meeting. To provide meaningful value, it is essential to shift your mindset from discovery to consultation. Coming back to the overarching objective of the consultation, which is to lead to future interactions, remember that can't be accomplished unless the DI feels they received meaningful value during the first meeting.

Additional Outcomes That MAY Need to Be Achieved

Depending upon the nature of your sale and your process, the following Outcomes may also be additions for your list.

- **Positioned your subject matter experts (SMEs).** If you have subject matter experts on your team who are differentiators that help you win deals, this Outcome should be considered for your list.

- **Toured their facility.** If seeing their facility affects your selling strategy or the solution you create, receiving a tour is an important Outcome.

- **Was introduced to others involved in the decision-making process.** In most cases, multiple DIs are involved in the decision-making process, and it's important to develop relationships with as many of them as possible.

- **Scheduled a demo.** If the consultation has gone well and a demo is the next step in your process, schedule it during the consultation when the energy and interest are high. If the person you are meeting with needs to coordinate with other DIs, put a tentative demo date on the calendar. You can always move the date if the other DIs are unavailable, but having a tentative date creates more certainty that it will occur and prevents you from having to chase them to schedule a date after the consultation.

- **Acquired the information needed to conduct an effective demo.** Related to the prior Outcome, if you are scheduling a demo, there's likely information you need to effectively perform the demo. Determine what that is so you can acquire that information during the consultation.

- **Scheduled a group presentation.** If the consultation has gone well and a presentation is the next step of your process, schedule it during the consultation for the same reasons you would for a demo. If they need to coordinate with other DIs, put a tentative group presentation date on the calendar. If you don't, the sales cycle will likely lengthen, and you run the risk of their interest in pursuing this further waning.

- **Acquired the information needed to conduct an effective group presentation.** Related to the prior Outcome, if you are scheduling a group presentation, there's likely information you need to properly handle that step. Just like with a demo, determine what that is so you can acquire that information during the consultation.

- **Received a referral to other parts of the company.** This Outcome is relevant if you sell to individual locations or divisions rather than entire corporate entities. Achieving this one exposes additional selling opportunities for you within the organization.

- **Received a referral to other companies or organizations.** This is a function of the meaningful value you provided during the consultation. If you have earned the right to ask for a referral during the consultation, you may have this one on your list.

- **Acquired information needed to construct a proposal.**
  If the next step following the consultation is to develop a
  proposal, then before the consultation, you should know what
  information you need to acquire during the consultation to
  achieve this Outcome.

- **Uncovered opportunities for other segments of your
  business.** If you represent one product line and have
  colleagues within your company who represent others, an
  Outcome to consider is identifying opportunities to sell those
  other product lines. If everyone achieves this throughout your
  sales organization, the entire group will have warm leads.

Expertise

Demonstrating expertise during consultations is another crucial
aspect of accomplishing the overarching objective of creating a
desire within your DIs to continue the relationship with you. Your DIs
will appreciate that you invested time in this mastery, and it can be
a major differentiator for you.

This set of Outcomes isn't just about possessing expertise. It's
about demonstrating the expertise during consultations, including
in the following:

- **The DI's role.** Mastery of DIs is a key to engagement and
  relationship building. The better you can convey that you
  understand them, their challenges, and their priorities, the
  better you can develop the engagement needed to establish
  trust and foster relationship development.

- **Their industry.** Industry mastery helps you have deeper
  conversations with DIs regarding best practices and trends.

- **Their company.** Investing time to understand their company's
  news, direction, and strategy allows you to convey that they
  are not the "sales call of the day," and it demonstrates genuine
  interest.

- **Your industry.** DIs want to work with salespeople with expertise in their respective industries because that expertise can help them creatively address their objectives and improve their business.

- **The solutions your company offers.** Salespeople who don't master what they are selling will struggle to develop solutions that get DIs excited to buy from them. Failing to achieve this objective during the consultation can be a deal killer.

Whew! As you read, there are a lot of Outcomes to consider for your Desired Consultation Outcomes list. Remember, if the consultation is designed correctly, future interactions will occur. That means, as I've mentioned, you must challenge yourself with your list of Desired Consultation Outcomes by selecting only the ones that must be achieved during the consultation.

This list of potential Outcomes will help you establish 95 percent or more of your foundational consultation strategy. The remaining 5 percent is custom to your sale.

Before proceeding to the next chapter, based on the consultation worksheet you downloaded and the content in this chapter, you should now have identified the criteria for a great first consultation with a specific Decision Influencer. The remainder of this book teaches you how to achieve each Outcome. The next step of the consultation strategy development process is creating a deal-qualification tool, which I present in the next chapter.

THE FIRST MEETING DIFFERENTIATOR: CONCEPT #2

The foundational consultation strategy identifies the Outcomes you want to achieve; these Outcomes become your definition of a successful first meeting.

CHAPTER 3

THE CRITICAL TOOL EVERY SALESPERSON NEEDS TO QUALIFY DEALS

Every salesperson dreams of standing among the elite—the rainmakers, the top earners, the ones who close deals at a pace others can only admire. Yet in the quest for excellence, many overlook a critical factor: the strategic investment of time.

Why Deal Qualification Matters. Time is the ultimate currency in sales. Every salesperson has exactly twenty-four hours in their day, and the difference between mediocrity and mastery often boils down to how they invest that time. Top performers don't squander it on pursuing unwinnable deals. One way they protect their most precious resource is by having a dedicated focus on deal qualifying throughout the sales process, especially during consultations. They treat time as a precious resource, and they guard it fiercely with one mantra burned into their minds:

> **If you're going to lose, lose early!**

Deal qualifying is one of the most underappreciated skills by both salespeople and executives. I coach my clients to embrace that mantra as I challenge them about the deals they are pursuing. Are you chasing a real opportunity, or is this nothing but a deal mirage? When I conduct pipeline analyses with clients, what often initially looks like a strong portfolio of potential deals is, in reality, sales vapor. While this often surprises the sales manager, the salespeople usually knew in their hearts that the deals were weak but continued pursuing them out of habit or hope. The harsh truth? Activity often gets confused with accomplishment, and deals that salespeople should've dropped early end up devouring hours, days, or even weeks.

Salespeople frequently tell me about deals they lost at the decision finish line. As we peel back the layers of what transpired during their deal pursuits, it turns out the deals weren't lost. They were never in the game. The DI never saw their solution as a viable option. Had the salespeople qualified the deals early on, they never would have wasted time pursuing them because there wasn't a significant alignment between the two companies. Interestingly, this is usually obvious to sales managers and salespeople during postmortem discussions, but that clarity doesn't usually exist while salespeople are pursuing the deals.

Think of those pursuit minutes as a deal investment both for the salesperson and the company. Why invest significant time in a deal you are unlikely to win at the prices you want? When you think of deal pursuits that way, your perspective will significantly shift about the method and importance of deal qualification and you will better mitigate your time risk. You will challenge every minute of a deal pursuit, wondering: Is this deal worth pursuing?

It doesn't always feel this way, but there are tons of deals to be had in your sales territory. If you chase the wrong deals, your competitors will win the right ones. I've always considered the first meeting my go/no-go decision point based on deal qualifying. I can't say it often enough: If you are going to lose, lose early!

The prior chapter guided you through a process to develop a Desired Consultation Outcomes portfolio for a first meeting with a specific Decision Influencer. The information acquired regarding Current Circumstance, Future Solution, and Decision Framework serves several purposes, most notably enabling you to qualify deals. While I do dedicate this chapter to deal qualification, remember that, as I mentioned in chapter 1, qualification can't be your sole purpose for the consultation. The first meeting cannot just be for the salesperson's benefit. In later chapters, I'll delve further into providing meaningful value to the DI during the first meeting.

The Two Deal-Qualification Scales

The word *prospect* is commonly used in the sales world, and it has many definitions. In my mind, until a deal is thoroughly analyzed with an affirmative qualification, the proper term to use is *suspect*. Deals graduate from suspect to prospect based on the qualification exercise. That exercise is not about making the deal fit your qualifying criteria but discovering *if* it does. And that requires introspective honesty. As painful as that is, sometimes the best decision is to walk away early on because the deal isn't likely to happen.

The subject of qualifying is not a new concept. But I have found that while sales managers preach the importance of qualifying to their salespeople, few provide a detailed deal-qualification benchmarking tool. As a result, sales managers say the word *qualify*, but their salespeople are not equipped with what they need to analyze their deals adeptly. In the prior chapter, I shared that when a company has not fully defined its great consultation criteria, salespeople are left to create their own definitions. In the same way, a lack of a documented, detailed deal-qualification benchmarking tool is one reason why the definitions of *prospect* and *suspect* are vastly different within the same organization. Each salesperson defines those using their own perspective. But when a sales organization has defined a deal-qualification framework, the salespeople are equipped to qualify consistently with eyes wide open, which leads them to focus on the right deal-pursuit opportunities.

The deal-qualification benchmarking tool salespeople need must empower them to qualify deals using two scales:

1. *Meaningful Value:* What are the attributes of the accounts that will perceive the most meaningful value in what you offer? In other words, will the DIs see you as a viable option for this deal?
2. *Win Probability:* What are the attributes of the deals with the greatest likelihood of coming to fruition? Stated another way, how likely are you to win this deal at the prices you want?

This deal-qualification benchmarking exercise is another reason why the consultation is the deal foundation. It's a deal pursuit milestone: a decision point for you to determine whether or not to pursue the deal further.

The Deal-Qualification Tool
Every Salesperson Must Have

The major flaw when salespeople are asked to qualify deals is they are not provided with a deal-qualification benchmarking tool. Qualify relative to what? That vagueness leads to arbitrary and inconsistent qualifying. What every salesperson needs is a tool I call a Target Client Profile (TCP). Before you jump to thinking, "He's just wordsmithing Ideal Client Profile," I assure you I'm not. The TCP tool is different from an Ideal Client Profile (ICP).

An ICP says, "If all the stars were to align, this is the kind of business we'd love to have." It's like a lottery ticket. There's a one-in-a-gazillion chance that a salesperson will stumble into this type of opportunity. If you look up the word *ideal* in the dictionary, you see it defined as "existing only in one's mind." That certainly isn't helpful for salespeople when attempting to qualify deals. In my experience, ICPs are usually vague and lack the specific information salespeople need to qualify their deals adeptly.

Unlike an ICP, a TCP is the practical, detailed deal-qualification benchmarking tool every salesperson needs because it clearly defines who will perceive the most meaningful value in what you sell and identifies the deals with the highest probability of coming to fruition. It helps salespeople make deal-investment time decisions based on two scales: Meaningful Value and Win Probability. A TCP gives salespeople a laser focus for their deal pursuits because they have clarity regarding what the right deal to invest their time in looks, feels, smells, and tastes like.

A TCP is not a one-size-fits-all for all the solutions you sell. Every solution you offer needs its own TCP because the criteria for meaningful value and win probability differ for each solution. The TCP doesn't dictate what deals your company will accept—it empowers salespeople to decide which deals are worth pursuing based on specific criteria. Think of the TCP as your personalized blueprint for deal qualification.

Taking a step back, deal qualifying isn't limited to the consultation. It should begin well before the consultation. It should start during your research before sending a prospecting email or making a phone call. Qualifying also continues past the consultation, constantly challenging yourself to look realistically at the viability of the deal.

But the ultimate line in the sand for deal qualification is the consultation, and qualifying the deal should be one of your Desired Consultation Outcomes. Of course, the level of qualification to be conducted during consultations varies from company to company and sale type to sale type.

In my prior books *Sales Differentiation* and *Sell Different!*, I provided background information on constructing a TCP. But since then, I have greatly enhanced the TCP tool and expanded its scope beyond determining who will perceive the most meaningful value in what you sell. It now also focuses on identifying win probability.

■

THE TARGET CLIENT PROFILE WORKSHOP

Before reading further, download my Target Client Profile template at **www.TargetClientProfile.com** and select one solution you sell to go through the TCP development exercise.

In the remainder of this chapter, I present each of the twelve TCP components and give examples of what may be included within each one. I've also summarized the main concepts for each component. It is important to note that some components may not be relevant for your sale type. If a component isn't relevant to your sale type, don't use it.

Let's develop your TCP for one solution you offer.

1. SIZE

(Units, locations, revenue, users, hires, employees, seats, etc.)

> *Meaningful Value:* What size account/opportunity would experience the most meaningful value from this solution?

> *Win Probability:* What size account/opportunity gives deals the greatest likelihood of coming to fruition?

For some sale types, size is a significant consideration regarding perceived meaningful value and win probability. If an account is too big or too small, some DIs may not perceive enough meaningful value for them to award you the deal at the prices you want. If size affects either of the two scales, document the size considerations in your TCP. If not, skip this portion.

2. LOCATION

(Where your brand is strong, where they are expanding, where your headquarters is located, a new market for you or them, etc.)

> *Meaningful Value:* Where would an account perceive the most meaningful value from this solution?

> *Win Probability:* Where would accounts/opportunities give deals the greatest likelihood of coming to fruition?

Location can also be an important factor affecting meaningful value and win probability. I've seen deals won because the Decision Influencers perceived tremendous meaningful value when a provider had a local office near theirs. I've also experienced solution types where location was irrelevant to whether they perceived meaningful value and had no effect on win probability at all. If location affects either of the two scales, document those in the TCP. If not, skip this portion.

3. BUSINESS TYPE

(Consumer, commercial, government, specific vertical markets, etc.)

> *Meaningful Value:* Which market segments would perceive the most meaningful value from this solution?

> *Win Probability:* Which market segments give deals the greatest likelihood of coming to fruition?

This component refers to selecting market segments on which the salespeople should focus. For example, if law firms perceive more meaningful value and provide a higher win probability than manufacturing ones, that should be captured in your TCP. One way to discern which markets to pursue is to look at NAICS (North American Industry Classification System) codes and identify specific vertical markets to include in your TCP.

4. INCUMBENT

(From whom they are buying currently, if they manage the function internally, if they have outsourced the function, etc.)

> *Meaningful Value:* In what situations would accounts perceive the most meaningful value from this solution?

> *Win Probability:* What situations give deals the greatest likelihood of coming to fruition?

A perspective to consider for your TCP is their current provider. Are there competitors you know you can easily beat and thus win deals at your desired prices? If so, add that to your TCP. If you have differentiators that a provider does not, and those offer meaningful value leading to a high win probability, document that information in this section of the TCP to "target" those deal types.

But "incumbent" doesn't just refer to the provider they are using today. It's their overall situation. For example, if you sell an outsourced-type solution, the question to ask yourself is: Are they more likely to perceive meaningful value if they are currently outsourcing the function or if they are handling it internally? This aspect is an important data point to address in the TCP if it affects perceived meaningful value and win probability.

Taking this topic a step further, there are two sale types: Takeaway and Demand Generation. I'll use a bathroom setting to distinguish between these two sale types.

Takeaway means they are buying a similar solution from one of your competitors. They are already buying toilet paper, but it's not from you. In this sale type, you are trying to lead them to purchase from you instead of their current provider.

Demand Generation means you have a new solution to an old problem. In a bathroom setting, it could be that you sell bidets as an alternative to toilet paper. Given your selected solution and those two sale types, address in your TCP which sale type this is relative to incumbency.

5. CIRCUMSTANCES AND GOALS

(Issues they want to address, goals they have identified, initiatives they have launched or plan to launch, etc.)

Meaningful Value: Accounts with which types of circumstances, goals, and initiatives perceive the most meaningful value from this solution?

Win Probability: Which circumstances, goals, and initiatives give deals the greatest likelihood of coming to fruition?

This section answers the question: What are they trying to accomplish relative to your solution? Weigh their answer on the Meaningful Value and Win Probability scales. For example, if one of their issues (circumstances) is international order turnaround time, which is a differentiator of yours, they would perceive meaningful value in your solution, increasing the deal win probability. Capture that circumstance in your TCP.

If their goal is cost reduction, which your solution addresses well, this could also be a criteria to include in the TCP.

6. DECISION DRIVERS

(New executive hired, expanding their footprint, regulatory change in their industry, workforce reduction/expansion, acquisition, etc.)

Meaningful Value: Accounts experiencing which types of events/changes would perceive the most meaningful value from this solution?

Win Probability: Which events/changes give deals the greatest likelihood of coming to fruition?

A Decision Driver is an event that motivates a Decision Influencer to take action. For example, a deal-energizing Decision Driver could be a newly hired executive who has decision-making authority for your solution. Think about what you are asking Decision Influencers to do. You're asking them to change what they are doing today and buy from you instead. Most people don't respond well to change. Often, you are asking them to change a decision they personally made, like which supplier to buy from, the process they follow, or the solution they implemented. However, new executives want to make their mark and are not tied to past decisions when they come into an organization. They want to make a fast, positive impression, leaving them more receptive to the options and alternatives you offer. But that window won't stay open forever. You need to engage with them within their first year in the role. After that, they own what is in place and are less likely to make a change.

With inbound leads, there is an inquiry motivation driver to explore. A lead comes in. You immediately call them because you know the first to respond to a lead will most likely win the deal. You get them on the phone, and they express interest in what you sell. Great! But it's clear they are not the decision maker. So now what?

Here's what many salespeople miss: They don't conduct an ITR Analysis to qualify the lead. ITR stands for Idea Task Recommendation. This qualification step is essential to conduct whenever you are not talking directly with a decision-maker.

Did they inquire because they had an idea they wanted to explore? Or, were they given a task to gather information for someone else? Were they asked to evaluate options and make a recommendation? These are three completely different scenarios that necessitate exploration.

The ITR analysis provides the clarity needed to identify the best next steps to advance the deal.

If a lead is an "I," meaning an Idea, the key is knowing how heavily influential this person is in the organization. Do they have enough influence in the organization to make this deal happen?

If the lead is a "T," meaning a Task, an understanding of who and what is driving this initiative is needed, with the goal of bringing that person into the conversation.

If the lead is an "R," meaning a Recommendation, an understanding of the criteria they will use to evaluate options is essential so you can share information with them to shape their decision criteria.

That's just a few examples of Decision Drivers to consider for your TCP. Think about the internal and external events that affect the perception of meaningful value and your win probability. It could be stock market performance, interest rates, expansion plans, etc.

7. CORPORATE ATTRIBUTES

(Financial health, forward thinking, receptive to alternative approaches, organizational structure, ownership structure, etc.)

> *Meaningful Value:* Companies with what types of corporate attributes would perceive the most meaningful value from this solution?

> *Win Probability:* Accounts with what types of corporate attributes give deals the greatest likelihood of coming to fruition?

Coming back to my prior point about change, does it take a forward-thinking organization that embraces innovation to perceive meaningful value in your solution, thus leading to a high win probability? If so, that's a point to address in your TCP.

If your solution addresses cost reduction, those accounts focused on improving their company's financial health could perceive meaningful value from your solution, making winning the deal highly likely.

8. BUYING PROCESS

(How they evaluate potential solutions, price buyer versus value buyer, how they make buying decisions, etc.)

Meaningful Value: Accounts with what type of buying processes would perceive the most meaningful value from this solution?

Win Probability: Accounts with what type of buying processes give deals the greatest likelihood of coming to fruition?

Their Buying Process is a significant TCP component that takes several aspects into consideration. For example, in some sale types, whether a lead is an inbound lead or comes from a salesperson's outbound engagement has a major impact on Win Probability. While salespeople love inbound leads, the Decision Influencers, in these cases, have often contacted multiple providers, making it a highly competitive deal. When the salesperson is the one who reached out and sparked interest, competition could be less or even nonexistent. The question is: Which of these two scenarios presents the best chance of winning the deal at the prices you want?

In chapter 1, I shared a favorite question of mine to ask salespeople: Who knows more about the world of potential solutions in your industry—you or the people you sell to? Every salesperson I asked said it was them. Taking that point a step further, DIs often don't know how to make an informed decision when buying your solution. That places the burden on your company to map out a buying journey so that they perceive meaningful value, which increases win probability. If they aren't open to that guidance, will you have a genuine opportunity to win the deal at the prices you want? That's also an important point to address in your TCP.

9. DECISION INFLUENCERS

(The initial person you meet with and their level of influence to affect change in the organization, the roles involved in the decision-making process, the role driving the decision, etc.)

> *Meaningful Value:* Which Decision Influencers would perceive the most meaningful value from this solution?

> *Win Probability:* Which Decision Influencers need to be involved for the greatest likelihood of a deal coming to fruition?

This TCP component addresses "the who" from several vantage points. Given the Meaningful Value and Win Probability scales, who should the salesperson initiate conversations with because they will have the greatest interest in the solution? From there, which DIs need to be involved for the deal to have a high likelihood of being won? Which DI do you want driving the decision? These are all factors to address in your TCP.

10. FUNDING

(Current spend level for a similar/related solution that you would displace, has already set a spend amount for a new solution, has clarity regarding funding for the investment, their level of influence to create available dollars, etc.)

> *Meaningful Value:* What amount of funding do they need to be prepared to invest to perceive the most meaningful value from this solution?

> *Win Probability:* What amount of funding do they need to be willing to invest for the greatest likelihood of a deal coming to fruition?

You'll notice I didn't title this component "budget." Budget is a limiting mindset. It means you are focused on a set quantity of dollars. Yet at some point in our lives, we all have bought something for more than our predetermined budget because we perceived enough meaningful value to justify the spending.

Plus, in my world, also true for many sale types, there's no established budget for what we sell. The question is whether the Decision Influencer perceives enough meaningful value to "find the dollars" for the solution. What this also means is, coming back to the previous component, you need to be working with those not constrained by budgets but rather with enough authority to create funding if they perceive enough meaningful value in a solution.

Deal-qualification benchmarking also necessitates understanding where the funds will come from if they want to pursue your solution. If they don't know how the deal would be funded, the salesperson should question the win probability and whether or not to invest more time in pursuing this deal.

11. REQUIREMENTS

(Quantity, customization, technology, operations, service, contract terms, pricing structure, online ordering, integration with their system, etc.)

> *Meaningful Value:* What types of requirements do they need to have to perceive the most meaningful value from this solution?
>
> *Win Probability:* What types of requirements give deals the greatest likelihood of coming to fruition?

When you first read "Requirements," I'm sure your mind immediately went to the negative side. But this is a positive component of the TCP. The concept is to identify a DI's requirements relative to the solution and look for meaningful value opportunities. For example, suppose they have international requirements, and you specialize in providing the solution globally. In that case, there is a strong chance they will perceive meaningful value, leading to a high win probability.

What DI requirements allow you to demonstrate enough meaningful value to make a deal highly likely to be won at your desired prices? That's the question to answer within this component.

12. DEAL BREAKERS

(Converse of the other Target Client Profile criteria and any other aspect that tells you this is not the right opportunity to pursue.)

> *Meaningful Value:* What indicators tell you they are unlikely to perceive meaningful value from this solution?

> *Win Probability:* Based on this solution, what indicators tell you there is a low likelihood of a deal coming to fruition?

The first eleven components of the TCP focused on the positive side of the deal pursuit: the DI's perception of meaningful value in the solution and the likelihood of a deal coming to fruition. The final component is to identify *Deal Breakers*. These indicators tell you to run from the deal as fast as possible because the DI does not perceive enough meaningful value to award you the deal at the prices you want.

A common Deal Breaker is a requirement to buy through an RFP, which often commoditizes the sale. I have several clients that agree to respond to RFPs only under certain conditions. For example, if they receive a blind RFP (one with no relationships with DIs), many of them decline to participate because there is a low likelihood of perceived meaningful value, leading to a low win probability.

Deal Breakers should be scrutinized as early as possible to maintain focus on the "lose early" mantra. For example, if having a consultation means getting on a plane or driving five hours, I highly suggest you qualify the opportunity for *Deal Breakers* before purchasing your airline ticket or jumping in the car.

In this component, identify attributes that indicate they will not perceive meaningful value, making a deal improbable. Also, list attributes that your company does not want.

Protecting Your Time Investment

As mentioned earlier, every solution your company offers needs a unique TCP due to the variance in criteria.

And remember, your TCP doesn't define which deals you will accept. It tells you where to focus your sales efforts based on the Meaningful Value and Win Probability scales. The TCP is the deal-qualification benchmarking tool that salespeople need to consistently qualify deals properly and ensure they invest their time wisely. When they use the term *prospect*, everyone in the company will know they have identified a strong match between your TCP and a potential deal.

Whenever a deal does not align with the TCP, internal conversations need to be had to determine whether the deal is worth pursuing both for you and your employer. *Lose early!* That mantra benefits your DI as well. No one has time to waste on something that won't happen. Your DIs will appreciate your stopping the process and informing them that there isn't a fit between the organizations.

Most salespeople are fundamentally optimistic and see the positive in every deal. With deal qualifying, I recommend having a pessimistic perspective and that you ask yourself: Why won't this deal happen? That approach challenges you to identify the strength of the matches (or lack thereof) between your TCP and the deal. That question also exposes deal vulnerabilities so you have the chance to address them. It forces you to remove the rose-colored glasses that dupe salespeople into chasing deals that are nothing but mirages so you can look at deals from an analytical perspective.

Based on your work in chapters 2 and 3, you now have defined Desired Consultation Outcomes and developed a Target Client Profile that serves as a qualification benchmarking tool. The next step of the consultation strategy development process is understanding what research and preparation is needed to conduct a masterful consultation. I present that strategy component in the next chapter.

THE FIRST MEETING DIFFERENTIATOR: CONCEPT #3

Use your Target Client Profile as a deal-qualification benchmarking tool to determine which deals should be pursued further and which ones should not.

CHAPTER 4

PREPARATION

YOUR KEY TO A MASTERFUL CONSULTATION

I n chapter 1, I compared a salesperson's consultation with a doctor's. In the medical field, doctors don't blindly walk into a consultation. Their medical school training provided foundational knowledge and skills, preparing them to conduct masterful consultations within their specialty. Their staff prepares them for each patient consultation with the information they need to personalize the experience.

Like doctors, salespeople need a two-step process to conduct a consultation that helps them achieve their Desired Consultation Outcomes. First, they must acquire a particular set of overarching knowledge and skills they'll use for all consultations. Second, they need to gather specific information to personalize the experience for each Decision Influencer.

Why is consultation preparation essential? Salespeople who invest time in this preparation gain several significant benefits:

1. Reduces the time it takes to have a substantive interaction.
2. Opens up directions the first meeting could take.
3. Ensures the DI receives meaningful value.
4. Serves as a deal-qualification step. (If you are going to lose, lose early!)

5. Allows salespeople to develop more insightful questions and share relevant information.
6. Makes DIs feel special, which leads to better engagement.

Let's start with the components of the overarching knowledge and skills salespeople need to prepare for masterful consultations: Decision Influencer Analysis and Other Players Analysis.

Decision Influencer Mastery

One of the Outcomes you likely selected is to demonstrate your expertise in the DI's role. This is a key to engagement and building relationships. The better you understand them, their challenges, and their priorities, the better you can develop the engagement needed to establish trust and foster a relationship. As my good friend Antarctic Mike says, "You have to understand them as a person, before you can see them as a prospect."

A fair expectation DIs have is that salespeople come to a consultation with an understanding of the DI's role. Failing to demonstrate that mastery means the first meeting is likely to fail to meet the definition of a consultation.

Developing that mastery used to be hard to do. It required hours and hours of research. Not anymore! The advent of artificial intelligence makes it easy for you to develop DI role mastery.

Most salespeople conduct consultations with the same group of job titles: CEOs, business owners, operations executives, etc. For each of them, mastery regarding their goals, objectives, concerns, and priorities is essential for a great consultation to be achieved. That mastery must be specific to the roles within each market segment because there will likely be variances.

Let's go through a workshop to develop Decision Influencer mastery.

■

DECISION INFLUENCER ANALYSIS WORKSHOP

Before proceeding, download my Decision Influencer Analysis worksheet at **www.DecisionInfluencerAnalysis.com**. At the top of the document, enter the Decision Influencer's title and market segment (for example, CFO—Manufacturing).

Step 1: *Select a Decision Influencer within a market segment with whom you conduct consultations.*

The goals, objectives, concerns, and priorities of CFOs in IT services may differ from those in other market segments. Learning this information used to take a lot of time to research. For this workshop, I'll use a manufacturing CFO as an example.

Step 2: *Create a prompt in ChatGPT requesting the analytical information you need for the selected Decision Influencer.*

My good friend Sam Richter helps salespeople master Generative AI to build more profitable businesses. He recommends using his Persona GUIDE principle to develop an effective prompt.

- G = What is the goal?

- U = Who is "us?"

- I = Who is the intended audience?

- D = How do you want the information delivered?

- E = In what environment is the information going to be received?

Based on Sam's Persona GUIDE, he created the following prompt for someone selling Customer Relationship Management

(CRM) software targeting CFOs to create an effective selling strategy:

> You are a leading business analyst and researcher with extensive expertise in understanding the specific goals, objectives, concerns, and priorities of various job titles within organizations. I am a salesperson at a CRM company, and I want to ensure that my solutions align with what is most important to CFOs in manufacturing organizations. Please help me by identifying the key goals, objectives, concerns, and priorities of CFOs within manufacturing organizations. I will use this information to shape my sales plan. Please let me know if you have any questions or need further clarification.

That prompt produced the following response from ChatGPT.

Key Goals, Objectives, Concerns, and Priorities of CFOs in Manufacturing Organizations

CFOs in manufacturing companies focus on financial stability, operational efficiency, and risk management. Their priorities include optimizing cash flow, reducing costs, improving financial forecasting, managing supply chain risks, and ensuring compliance. They are highly data-driven and seek tools that provide real-time visibility into financial performance, streamline processes, and improve profitability.

Below are the key focus areas for CFOs in manufacturing and how a CRM solution could align with their needs:

1. Optimizing Cash Flow and Working Capital Management

- CFOs need to ensure strong cash flow by managing receivables, payables, and inventory efficiently.

- They seek better forecasting to anticipate financial needs and avoid liquidity issues.

CRM Relevance:

- Integration with an Enterprise Resource Planning (ERP) system allows real-time tracking of sales, receivables, and outstanding payments.

- CRM-driven forecasting helps predict revenue trends and align cash flow strategies.

- Automated reminders reduce late payments and improve cash cycle management.

2. Reducing Operational Costs and Improving Efficiency

- Cost control is a major priority; CFOs look to cut unnecessary expenses without sacrificing quality.

- CFOs seek technology that eliminates inefficiencies and manual processes.

CRM Relevance:

- Eliminates duplicate data entry by syncing with ERP, reducing administrative overhead.

- Automates sales workflows, reducing labor costs and improving productivity.

- Provides analytics to identify cost-saving opportunities in sales and customer management.

3. Enhancing Financial Forecasting and Data-Driven Decision-Making

- CFOs must provide accurate financial forecasts to support budgeting and strategic planning.

- They need real-time insights into revenue trends, profitability, and market conditions.

CRM Relevance:

- AI–powered analytics improve revenue forecasting accuracy.
- CRM tracks sales pipeline data, providing CFOs with real-time insights into future revenue.
- Integration with ERP ensures financial projections are based on actual sales trends.

4. Managing Supply Chain and Inventory Costs

- CFOs oversee inventory costs and ensure optimal stock levels to avoid overstocking or stockouts.
- They aim to enhance vendor negotiations and reduce supply chain risks.

CRM Relevance:

- Sales data integration helps CFOs forecast demand and optimize inventory levels.
- CRM insights improve vendor performance tracking and contract negotiations.
- Real-time sales order tracking minimizes production delays and unnecessary inventory costs.

5. Ensuring Regulatory Compliance and Audit Readiness

- Manufacturing CFOs must comply with financial regulations, tax laws, and industry-specific mandates.
- They need reliable data and reporting tools to prepare for audits.

CRM Relevance:

- Provides centralized customer and financial data for accurate compliance reporting.

- Maintains audit trails, ensuring financial transparency and regulatory adherence.

- Automates documentation, reducing compliance risks and simplifying audits.

6. Maximizing Profitability and Pricing Strategies

- CFOs must balance competitive pricing with margin protection.

- They seek insights into pricing trends and customer profitability.

CRM Relevance:

- CRM analytics provide visibility into customer behavior and purchasing patterns.

- Helps CFOs optimize pricing strategies based on real-time sales and margin data.

- Identifies the most profitable customers, helping prioritize sales efforts.

7. Improving Customer Retention and Lifetime Value

- CFOs recognize that retaining existing customers is more cost-effective than acquiring new ones.

- They want to ensure strong customer relationships for recurring revenue.

CRM Relevance:

- Tracks customer engagement and purchase history to identify retention risks.

- Enables personalized outreach and follow-ups to enhance customer relationships.

- Helps CFOs analyze churn patterns and develop strategies to maximize lifetime value.

By focusing on these key priorities, you can tailor your CRM sales strategy to directly address CFO concerns and demonstrate how your solution impacts financial performance and operational efficiency.

That response took a matter of seconds. In the past, that analysis would have taken several hours to complete. Always validate the information you gather from AI tools by doing your own research. When creating prompts, ask ChatGPT to check the internet for the most current information. While AI tools can be an enormous time saver, since they are new tools with imperfect technology, they can sometimes provide inaccurate or erroneous information.

While having this information is a great start, not all of it is relevant to your sale. You will need to parse through it to extract the pertinent information for your sale, leading to the filtering required during the next step.

Step 3: *For each of the returned goals, objectives, concerns, and priorities, ask yourself if it is something that your solution can address for this DI.*

Using the example of manufacturing CFOs, ChatGPT returned twenty-four of what I call "keeping DIs up at night" factors. Of course, what you sell will not likely be able to address all of them. Review the list that ChatGPT produced, select the ones your solution can address, and enter them on the left side of the Decision Influencer Analysis worksheet.

Step 4: *For those aspects your solution addresses, identify how it addresses each one.*

Let's say that after reviewing the twenty-four "keeping DIs up at night" factors, you determined that your solution addresses eight of them and entered them in the worksheet. For each of those eight, the next step is defining how you can address them.

For example, let's say your solution addresses "Cost Control and Efficiency," which was one of the factors provided by ChatGPT. Ask yourself: How does my solution address cost control and efficiency? Enter that information in the corresponding cell in the right-hand column of the worksheet and repeat for all the factors.

You've now created a Decision Influencer Analysis for a specific role. This new sales tool helps you develop insightful questions to ask the DI and select relevant differentiators to share during the consultation. Create a Decision Influencer Analysis worksheet for each role you engage with during consultations.

Other Players Mastery

The Decision Influencer Analysis is step 1 of overarching consultation preparation, but there is more work to be done. Step 2 is conducting an Other Players Analysis.

I used to refer to this consultation preparation tool as a Competitor Analysis, but a CEO client of mine changed my perspective. In his company, he banned the use of the word *competitor*, both internally and externally because he felt that word inaccurately elevated the status of the others in their space. He said, "Selling is hard enough as it is. Why make it more difficult by unnecessarily elevating their perceived status?" The expression he used, which I have embraced, is "Other Players."

I've seen Other Players Analysis done in various ways that overcomplicate the exercise. I prefer to make this exercise both simple and effective.

Let's go through a workshop for Other Players mastery.

■

OTHER PLAYERS ANALYSIS WORKSHOP

Before proceeding, download my Other Players Analysis worksheet at **www.OtherPlayersAnalysis.com**.

Step 1: *Make a list of the other players commonly encountered during your deal pursuits.*

There is no need to list every other player. Focus on the primary ones you encounter when selling. Select one other player for the next steps of this analysis and enter their name at the top of the worksheet.

Step 2: *Identify the reasons why you win when competing against this other player for a deal.*

In short, the question to ask yourself is: Relative to this other player, why do you win? The question isn't why you win in generalities. It's specific to this other player. Some examples may include: product quality, breadth of offering, cost basis, reputation, technology, and contract terms. Enter that information in the worksheet. When entering the information, use the following format: what you offer, what the other player offers, why what you offer is more advantageous to DIs, and a reason why you win.

Step 3: *Identify the reasons why the other player wins when competing against you.*

Ask yourself, Relative to this *other player*, why do they win? Just like the examples provided for reasons you win, the list of reasons why they win may include product quality, breadth of offering, cost basis, reputation, technology, and contract terms. Enter that information in the worksheet. When entering the information, use the following format: what *Other Player* offers, what you offer, and why what they offer is more advantageous to DIs as a reason why they win.

You may have noticed that "price" is omitted from my list of examples. That is intentional. Price should never be a listed reason in this analysis. It's a cop-out. Salespeople often cite price as a reason they don't win deals when, in reality, that wasn't the cause for the loss. They lost due to their inability to demonstrate enough meaningful value (differentiate) in their solution to justify the presented price.

However, you'll notice the reason "cost basis" given as an example relative to the selected *Other Player*. For instance, if they manufacture their products outside the country, which reduces their cost, they may be able to sell at a lower price point than you for the same solution. That is not the same as saying they win due to low price. This is a data point that should be documented in the worksheet.

You've now created an *Other Players Analysis* for this specific *Other Player*. Like the DI Analysis, this new sales tool helps you develop insightful questions to ask the DI and enables you to select relevant differentiators to share during the consultation, but in this case, it is relative to this specific *Other Player*. As you compete against additional *Other Players*, create an analysis worksheet for each one of them.

Solution Mastery

There is one more overarching preparation step needed for your consultations, which is Solution Mastery.

While this may seem obvious, salespeople must master what they are selling. I say this may seem obvious, but I've encountered more than my fair share of salespeople who have not mastered what they sell. Without that mastery, the likelihood of achieving the Desired Consultation Outcomes is slim to none.

You can develop solution mastery by doing the following:

- Reviewing case studies.
- Interviewing sales team colleagues.
- Talking with non-salespeople in your organization.
- Reading your website.
- Reviewing your marketing materials.
- Researching your industry to know trends.

In chapter 1, I shared a favorite question of mine: Who knows more about the world of potential solutions in your industry? If you want that answer to be you (which it must be to deliver effective consultations), it is impossible to overinvest in mastering the solutions you sell.

During consultations, just as you will ask questions of the DI, they will ask questions of you. How you respond reflects your consultation preparation. You need to be prepared to answer two types of questions: Fair Game and Beyond Your Pay Grade.

- **Fair Game.** A DI asks this question type and expects you to provide accurate answers on the spot. If you cannot, you come across as unprepared, which tarnishes the relationship. What are considered Fair Game questions vary for each sale type. An example of this question type is: What hours are your client services team accessible? It is fair for the DI to expect the salesperson at a consultation to know that answer.
- **Beyond Your Pay Grade.** The DI may also ask this question type. You may not know the answer off the top of your head because the question is technical in nature. Technical doesn't necessarily mean about technology. It can be about intimate details requiring detailed knowledge. It is perfectly acceptable for you not to have immediate answers to these questions. But there is still an important DI expectation for these questions.

They expect you to know how to acquire the information and that you will share it with them in a timely manner.

Beyond-your-pay-grade questions are about custom options regarding your solution that can be operations or technology related, such as: Can you develop an integration using this technology schema that provides updates every six seconds for thirty-eight data points?

The appropriate response for this question type is: "That's a great question, and I know who to ask in my company for the answer. I'll get back to you tomorrow with their response." Make sure you deliver on "tomorrow."

Personalizing the Consultation

The three areas we just went over—Decision Influencer Analyses, Other Player Analyses, and Solution Mastery—parallel doctors' education in medical school: This is the general information needed for consultations. Like doctors, however, when you prepare for individual consultations, you need to go to the next level: personalizing the experience.

The Personalized Consultation

Regardless of who you are meeting with for a consultation, they expect personalization. It's a requirement!

If you come across like this is just another consultation and the impression you give is that you could have used your meeting content with anyone, you will fail in the overarching objective of piquing a high enough level of interest so that the DI wants to continue interacting with you after the consultation.

In addition, this research is a component of qualifying. When you review your Desired Consultation Outcomes list, which defines a great consultation, you'll see that you can achieve some of those through research before the first meeting. Research also gives you an opportunity to stay true to the mantra: If you are going to lose, lose early!

Imagine you are preparing for a first meeting with Henry Michaels, CFO of JSD Manufacturing, who currently buys from ABC Services. Here are the personalization preparation steps that you could use (*not* in order or priority).

- **Relationship History.** While most CRMs are not used as religiously as sales managers would like, there is often a wealth of information to be found in those systems. Hopefully, you searched your CRM before prospecting. But if you have not, this is the time to do so. You should understand the history of all the relationships between your company and JSD Manufacturing. It would be embarrassing to find out during a consultation that they are a former client or that your company already sells to a division of theirs. If they are a former client, research internally to learn why they left. If you currently work with a division of theirs, find out everything you can about the current relationship.
- **Social Media Search.** Review Henry Michaels's and JSD Manufacturing's profiles on LinkedIn and other major social media platforms. To personalize the consultation, you should look at his profile for any commonalities between you and Henry. Perhaps you went to the same school as him, or his former employer is your client. This information makes for a bonding conversation and communicates that you did your homework in preparation for the first meeting.
- **Google Search.** Conduct a Google search of "JSD Manufacturing," focusing on company news. If, for example, you find out that they are expanding into Europe and your solution is available worldwide, this can become a discussion

point during the consultation. Again, it affirms that you prepared for the consultation.

- **Website Search.** Look for news, executive bios, company values, mission statement, partners, etc. Let's say JSD Manufacturing's website emphasizes their client experience and that's something your company also takes pride in. That becomes another discussion topic for the first meeting.
- **Industry Intelligence.** I'm a big fan of developing industry relationships for several reasons, including gaining consultation intelligence. You'd be amazed at how much information you can gather from providers who do not compete with you. This type of information can be extremely useful in helping you develop a personalized consultation strategy.

  Back in the day, when I was in the technology training industry, my salespeople would gather intel from our Microsoft representative when they pursued corporate accounts. Because he often had insights about the technology industry and Microsoft's competitors that we didn't have access to, insights that paved the way for great consultations.

- **Their Competitors Search.** What you are looking for here are opportunities to help JSD Manufacturing get a leg up on their other players by leveraging your solution. How do you find out who their competitors are? Again, use an AI tool like ChatGPT and create a prompt: "Who are JSD Manufacturing's biggest competitors today?" It may not be entirely accurate, but you can determine that as you visit those identified competitors' websites. Remember, when using AI, make sure you do further research (for example, visit the identified competitors' websites) to validate the information.
- **Decision Influencer Analysis.** Study your CFO Decision Influencer Analysis for the manufacturing marketing segment so you come across as knowledgeable about Henry's role as a manufacturing CFO. Based on the analysis, develop

questions to ask him. For example, many manufacturing CFOs tell us they are heavily focused on cost reduction for their manufacturing processes. Where does that fall in your list of priorities for the upcoming year? A question such as this communicates that this is not a random first meeting; it's one you prepared to have.

- **Other Players Analysis.** Review the Other Players Analysis for ABC Services, from whom JSD Manufacturing is currently buying, to find their vulnerabilities and be able to position your differentiators compellingly during the consultation.
- **Solution Expertise.** Based on all your research, consider the likely solution you'll discuss during the consultation and be ready to address Henry's Fair Game questions.

Consultation Game Plan

If you followed this consultation preparation plan, you now have a wealth of information to use. Here is what to do with that information.

- Review your Desired Consultation Outcomes list and see if you can qualify any of the identified factors before the consultation.
- Identify the differentiators that are most likely to be relevant during the consultation.
- Develop insightful questions demonstrating what you have researched to prepare for the consultation.
- Select information that should be shared during the consultation.
- Identify actions to take before, during, and after the consultation based on your research relative to your list of Desired Consultation Outcomes.

Consultations don't go as expected for one primary reason: the salesperson's lack of preparation. We expect doctors to be fully prepared for consultations. Why not have that same expectation of salespeople? We should!

In the next chapter, you will learn a critical consultation concept that, with proper preparation, makes for an outstanding consultation. Get ready to learn how to leverage the Deal Energizer!

THE FIRST MEETING DIFFERENTIATOR: CONCEPT #4

A major factor contributing to a consultation's success is the salesperson's preparation.

CHAPTER 5

EMOTION
THE DEAL ENERGIZER

O n December 22, 2022, my dad passed away. He had spent his entire career in accounting and banking. Given his professional background, he was always the one to prepare my parents' taxes. As his health deteriorated, my mom urged him to hire a CPA to handle this for them. It took several years of her urging, but he finally agreed to it in 2022.

After my dad passed away, I began managing my mom's finances and worked with her accountant to prepare her taxes for the April 2023 deadline. The accountant filed the return accurately and on time . . . and I FIRED him. Lee, you just said he submitted everything correctly and on time. Why did you fire him? That makes no sense!

I'll explain. Whenever my mom, sister, or I talked with the accountant, he was disrespectful and made us feel like idiots (and that's an understatement). Despite having known my father for years, he showed no sensitivity to the situation and no understanding of the emotions we were experiencing. The three of us despised talking with him because of how he made us feel. He lost this account not because of his work quality but because he lacked what I call Empathetic Expertise.

"People will forget what you said, people will forget what you did, but people will never forget how you made them feel." That famous expression certainly rang true with this accountant, and it's an important message for every salesperson to take to heart.

Empathetic Expertise

Dictionary.com defines *empathy* as the psychological identification with or vicarious experience of another's emotions, thoughts, or attitudes. In other words, an empathetic person understands and appreciates the emotions of another person. Top salespeople recognize the impact of emotion on decision-making and the importance of empathetic mastery. They invest time to understand their Decision Influencers' emotions so they can appropriately interact with them.

You've probably heard that people buy from those they like and trust. That expression is partially true. There are four criteria people use to judge whom to buy from. Like and trust are two. Two other reasons are that people buy from

1. those they feel are experts in the solution they are selling, and
2. those who demonstrate Empathetic Expertise when interacting with them.

A salesperson with product mastery who is unlikable, untrustworthy, and fails to show appreciation for the Decision Influencer's emotions sells nothing. A salesperson who demonstrates Empathetic Expertise, however, comes across as more likable and more trusted, giving the impression of having product mastery whether or not they possess it.

Those salespeople can meaningfully differentiate themselves from the competition based on how they make others feel during interactions, and differentiation is a major factor in winning deals. How you make people feel is a significant differentiator that affects buying decisions!

How do you know if someone has Empathetic Expertise? The measurement gauge is quite simple. It comes down to whether the DI *feels* these three words: "You get me." Think about those with whom you enjoy doing business. A primary reason is that you feel they understand you and thus you feel good about interacting with them. They get you. More specifically, they understand your wide array of emotions regarding the issues what they sell addresses, and they convey that understanding to you. It's not price that keeps you coming back but rather how you feel when you engage with them. That's why top salespeople have relationships rather than transactions.

Let's contrast my accountant experience with one where the service provider created a completely different experience in another difficult circumstance. In August 2024, we had to say goodbye to our amazing dog, Rocky. We adopted him when he was six months old and had a great life with him for fifteen years. The last year was progressively challenging because he was diagnosed with thyroid cancer. His health deteriorated to a point where there was no decision left for us to make. The time had come . . .

We decided to have the euthanasia process done in our home to make it as comfortable as possible for him. Our veterinarian did not offer this service. But we found several others that provided only euthanasia services. As I did my research through my tears, I was surprised by how many of them there were. A lot! How would I determine which one to select?

Our veterinarian referred one, so I started with them. The conversation I was about to have would be the toughest one of my life. I struggled (and failed) to keep my composure as I spoke with their intake professional, but she made the conversation as easy as possible. She spoke to me ever so softly and asked questions gently. She never referred to Rocky as a dog but as "your sweet baby." It was clear to me that she understood all the emotions I was feeling at that moment. She got me! And I contracted with them immediately. She was likable. Even though she wasn't the veterinarian who would provide the service, I trusted her, which made me trust the practice. She had solution expertise because she had a clear answer to all my questions. Most importantly, she conveyed that she understood all the emotions I was experiencing in that painful moment.

There are three tools salespeople have in their toolbox to convey Empathetic Expertise:

1. The questions they ask.
2. The information they share visually and verbally.
3. The actions they take before, during, and after the interaction.

All three tools are not needed in all circumstances. You have to select the proper tools for the situation to convey that you understand their numerous emotions. Also important is how you use the tools. With the veterinary practice, it wasn't just the questions she asked but the tone of her voice when asking the questions that led me to select them.

Years ago, I consulted with an upscale vacation travel agency. Their agents (aka salespeople) did not make outbound calls; they fielded only inbound inquiries. During my first coaching session with them, I asked the group: "What is the first thing you say when you start a conversation with an inbound caller?" Some said they asked how they heard about the agency or asked qualifying questions.

After listening to several of their conversation starters, I asked them how they thought these inbound callers were feeling at that moment. The most prevalent emotion the group mentioned was *excitement*. Remember, this was a vacation travel agency. As a follow-up, I asked the group: "What if you started the conversation, after hearing they wanted to plan a vacation, by saying with high energy: 'That's fantastic! Where were you thinking of going?'"

They tried that conversation opener for a week, and then we met again. Every travel agent said that that little expression—"That's fantastic!"—as a conversation opener, completely changed the dynamic of the overall experience. Callers were friendlier and more open about sharing information. The call felt less like an interview and more like a conversation. Most importantly, as they developed their Empathetic Expertise over time, they noticed an increase in their conversion rates.

Logic Versus Emotion

One of the oldest and most accepted sales concepts is:

People buy based on emotion and justify their decisions with logic.

You've heard this expression if you've been in sales for as little as a week. I challenge you to find a decision-making study or a sales expert who disagrees with that statement. You won't find one.

In 2024, my wife, Sharon, introduced me to a TV series called *The Irrational*. Great show! It tells the story of a behavioral scientist with specialized expertise in human decision-making who uses that expertise to help the FBI solve cases. The show is based on the *New York Times* bestselling book *Predictably Irrational* and its author, Dan Ariely, a behavioral psychologist. In this book, Ariely shares several studies about how people make decisions, which I found fascinating, given what I do for a living. As you can probably imagine, his studies support the concept that people make decisions based on emotion and justify those decisions with logic. I immediately became a fan of Ariely, reached out to him, and asked him to contribute a section to this chapter, which he graciously agreed to do.

From Ariely:

> One study that demonstrates that people make decisions based on emotions started by showing people two pictures of two different faces and asking them which one they liked more. After people indicated which one they liked more, the researcher took away both pictures, presented one of them back to the participant, and asked: "Why did you say that you like this one more?" The participants then gave their reasons for liking that picture more.
>
> The participants didn't know that sometimes the researcher showed them the picture that they did not like more, the one they liked less. Interestingly, in most cases, the participants did not realize that the researchers showed them the picture they liked less. Even more importantly, they kept giving reasons for liking that picture more. The reasons given were emotional not logical.

What these results show is that we make choices, but these choices can be disconnected from the stories we tell ourselves afterward. In other words, we make decisions based on emotion, not logic.*

If you have not read the book *Predictably Irrational*, I highly recommend you do! It will help you better understand how your buyers make decisions so you can adjust your selling approach accordingly.

But let's take the emotional impact on decision-making a step further with this concept:

---

* P. Johansson, et al. "Choice Blindness and Preference Change: You Will Like This Paper Better If You (Believe You) Chose to Read It!" *Journal of Behavioral Decision Making* 27, no. 3 (2013): 281–289, https://doi.org/10.1002/bdm.1807.

Emotion is the deal energizer. Deals primarily based on logic are likely to stall out.

Let me put this another way.

Decision-making is emotional. It doesn't matter what you sell. The decision-making process is emotional. That's why if you have only logical conversations and don't arouse a Decision Influencer's emotions during consultations, the deal has no life and is likely to fizzle out.

The flaws of logic-based deals become evident when the DI delays decisions until sometime in the future (which you know is never) or the DI ghosts you (meaning they stop responding to your outreach).

If only I had a nickel for every time a frustrated salesperson said, "Lee, I don't understand. I had great conversations with the prospect, but the deal went nowhere." When I ask them about the tenor of the conversations, they almost always say they were having logic-based discussions only. Logic won't energize your deals. Only emotion does.

If you want people to do something, they need to feel something.

That statement is valid for every step in the sales process: prospecting, consultations, presentations, demos, etc. The most common reason deals never advance past the current step is that the DIs didn't experience a high enough level of emotion.

For most people, if you walk past a bowl of chocolate candies, the logical side of your brain says, "Keep walking. You know that's not healthy for you." Then the emotional side counterargues, "Grab some! It'll make you feel good." Which side wins? I don't need to tell you the answer. You know. The emotional side convinces the logical side that "you'll walk it off later and burn the calories." Emotion drives action!

In 1984, Michelin, the car tire manufacturer, launched an ad campaign designed to spark emotion, and it worked. The ads showed a baby beside a tire with the text line: "Michelin. Because so much is riding on your tires."

Consider the logic and emotion spectrum. This campaign was entirely an emotional ploy. It made people experience the emotion of protecting their family: If you want them to be safe, you'll install Michelin tires on your car. The ad didn't talk about quality, features, or functions, all logic topics. They aroused a high level of emotion, *driving* car owners to buy their products.

Recently, a client contracted with me to deliver a keynote talk in California, preceded by a book signing. I caught an early morning flight from Minneapolis and arrived at my hotel around 2 p.m., but something was amiss. There was a line of protesters picketing along the front of the hotel. As I checked in, I noticed a posting at the front desk explaining that their hotel workers were on strike and the hotel had limited services. Tired from the flight and since I had a few hours before my book signing, I went up to my room to take a nap. But that was quickly interrupted. As soon as I arrived in my room, I heard garbage cans banging and horns blowing. It was the picketers. Crud! I put in my AirPods to drown out the sound, but it didn't work. Then I heard police sirens. *Yes! Thank goodness. There will now be quiet.* But the sirens weren't getting closer, nor were they getting farther away. I looked out the window to see what was going on. To my surprise, the police hadn't arrived. The siren was another toy the picketers had in their bag of tricks.

Why were the picketers making all this noise? They wanted to anger the guests so that they would complain to management, and then management would be motivated to address the picketers' demands. Irritated guests canceled their reservations and grumbled to management about the noise. The strikers aroused emotion to get action. And it worked!

Emotional Jurisprudence

If you have read my prior books or watched my videos, you know I'm a huge fan of the original *Law & Order* TV show. (Given that I also love *The Irrational*, you can probably tell my television show preferences.)

When Sharon and I were dating, I'd go to her apartment on Wednesday nights, and we would watch new episodes together. I know what you're thinking. We were wild and crazy kids back then!

I was thrilled when, in 2021, they brought the show back in a reboot. During one episode in season two, the prosecutor was very frustrated with how his case was progressing. He felt he had all the facts he needed to convict, but the expressions on the jurors' faces told him his case was in trouble. Given his concerns about the case, the prosecutor walked the district attorney through his case. When he finished, the district attorney responded, "The problem with your case is it's all fact, no heart, and the jury isn't buying it." That expression struck a chord with me. Much to my wife's chagrin, I had to rewind it five times to ensure I heard it correctly.

In other words, what the DA communicated was "All logic. No emotion. No sale!" That got me thinking about a potential parallel between attorneys and salespeople. Do attorneys engage emotions to affect jury decisions? While *Law & Order* says it's "ripped from the headlines," obviously it isn't a legitimate source to cite. Intrigued by the topic, I interviewed a judge, a prosecutor, a litigator, and a litigator trainer in search of an answer, and the conversations I had with them were fascinating.

When I interviewed Wade Kish, a twenty-two-year prosecutor, he talked about emotionally connecting with the jury. His objective is to motivate the jury to move from having the *ability* to convict to having the *desire* to convict. Only one way that happens: by engaging the jurors' emotions.

His point about shifting from "the *ability* to convict to having the *desire* to convict" is pure sales gold. Decision Influencers have the *ability* to contract with us. During consultations, we need to lead DIs down a path so they have a *desire* to contract with us. How does that happen? We need to adeptly engage their emotions. Dry facts alone won't do it.

Further making that point, Jesse Wilson, a litigator trainer, said that some attorneys focus on facts and hope emotions emerge, which is backward and ineffective. He coaches attorneys to think about how they want the jury to *feel* after each phase of the case. Wilson goes so far as to tell attorneys they shouldn't take a case if they can't get excited about it. I say the same thing to salespeople: If you can't get excited about the solutions you sell, go sell something else.

Kish shared an example of an emotional engagement technique he uses. "If I have a firefighter on the witness stand, I'm asking questions that make the jury *feel* like they were in the fire with the firefighter. I'm asking questions like 'What did you *feel* when you first entered the building?' I'm turning facts into emotional situations. I want the jury to experience the heat of the flames."

Kish also talked about jury selection. Part of a prosecutor's evaluation process is determining whom they can connect with emotionally. This also applies to the sales world. We need to work with Decision Influencers who can become passionate about what we sell. For example, if you sell a solution that reduces costs, CFOs can become excited because that is their focus. Mid-level managers are not held accountable for profitability, couldn't care less about reducing costs, and won't get fired up about the topic.

Before becoming a judge, Attorney Elizabeth Frizell was a criminal trial lawyer. As a trial lawyer, she wanted the jury to feel the experience of her witnesses. *That could have been me.* She talked about engaging the senses with questions like: "What did it smell like?" "What did you hear?" "What did it feel like?" Each of these is designed to arouse jury emotions. Coming back to what Kish said: having the *desire* to convict.

Why Salespeople Don't Engage Emotions

Like salespeople, attorneys appreciate the importance of emotional engagement in decision-making. Unlike attorneys, however, most salespeople don't engage emotions, at least not at a high enough level to energize their deals. If you observe most sales interactions, particularly how salespeople handle consultations, the conversations are entirely logic-based, with little to no emotion aroused. Salespeople ask only fact-based questions like: "How many of these do you use?" "When would you like to make a change?" "Who else would be involved in evaluating solution options?" While salespeople need these answers, logic-based questions cannot be your sole questioning approach. You need emotional engagement.

The sales profession pokes fun at car salespeople for all the ugly historical experiences buyers have had when purchasing vehicles. But these salespeople do something better than most others. They have mastered how to engage buyer emotions. When you arrive at a car dealership and walk into the showroom, the salesperson wants to get you behind the wheel as quickly as possible for a test drive. They adjust the seat so you are comfortable. They set the temperature just the way you like it and put your favorite tunes on the radio. Their objective is simple: to make you FEEL like you already own the car. They are looking for your smile, telling them you LOVE the vehicle. Once you smile, they know they can energize the deal and leverage your emotions to do it. Emotion drives action!

Why don't all salespeople engage emotions? For years, I sought an answer to that question. Every salesperson on the planet knows the sales concept that *people buy based on emotion and justify their decisions with logic*, but shockingly, few salespeople put it into practice. I couldn't understand why. Then it finally hit me. I thought about when my sons were little and learning to play baseball. Coaches told them to hit home runs, but that didn't happen unless coaches also taught the techniques to do it.

Sales leaders preach the importance of emotional engagement, but if no one teaches the salespeople how to do it, all you get is head nods. Nothing changes in their selling approach.

We are going to fix this now. The following section presents my Empathetic Expertise Emotional Transition workshop. This workshop guides you through the steps that lead you to become a master of emotional engagement. Let's get started!

EMPATHETIC EXPERTISE
EMOTIONAL TRANSITION WORKSHOP

Before proceeding, download my Empathetic Expertise worksheet at **www.EmpatheticExpertiseWorkshop.com** to follow the steps below.

Step 1: Foundation.

Select one solution you sell, one market segment it is sold to, and one Decision Influencer you would meet with for a consultation. For example, a performance management system (solution) meeting with a staffing company's (market segment) general manager (Decision Influencer). The reason for these selections is that the set of emotions varies from solution to solution, market segment to market segment, and DI to DI.

Step 2: Issues Addressed.

Make a list of all the issues your selected solution addresses for the chosen DI. Pick only issues that the selected DI cares about. The best way to identify these issues is by reviewing the Decision Influencer Analysis workshop you completed in chapter 4.

For example, if you chose a CFO as your DI for the workshop and one of your solution's attributes is a breadth of colors, the issue of "color flexibility" is likely irrelevant to the CFO because they are not usually concerned about color flexibility. Their focus is on the solution's financial impact. Examples of the types of issues to consider for your list are as follows:

- Productivity
- Efficiency
- Profitability
- Revenue

- Staffing
- Quality
- Accuracy
- Speed

- Compliance
- Flexibility
- Pricing structure
- Payment terms
- Payment options
- Cost reduction
- Warranty
- Maintenance

- Automation
- Integration
- Ease of use
- Breadth of solution types
- Durability
- Installation
- Ordering
- Delivery

Step 3: Pre-Consultation Emotional State.

For each issue you listed in step 2, there is a way (commonly multiple ways) the selected DI feels about it *before* a first meeting with you. How do they feel about each issue *before* the consultation and why do they feel that way? In other words, in this step, identify all the emotions your selected DI feels about the issues you address and the reasons why they feel that way before interacting with you.

Using the earlier example of a staffing GM and the performance management system, how does the GM feel about "performance" in their facility? Perhaps they are *frustrated* that they are not meeting staffing targets and, as a result, not receiving their performance bonuses.

Here is a list of common DI emotions to contrast with the issues listed in step 2.

COMMON DECISION INFLUENCER EMOTIONS

EMOTION TYPE		
POSITIVE	NEGATIVE	NEUTRAL
■ Confident	■ Accountable	■ Accepting
■ Curious	■ Afraid	■ Apathetic
■ Empowered	■ Angry	■ Complacent
■ Energized	■ Concerned	■ Detached
■ Euphoric	■ Confused	■ Disinterested
■ Excited	■ Defeated	■ Dispassionate
■ Happy	■ Disappointed	■ Indifferent
■ Informed	■ Envious	■ Nonchalant
■ Inspired	■ Exposed	■ Resigned
■ Interested	■ Frustrated	■ Satisfied
■ Intrigued	■ Neglected	■ Unconcerned
■ Motivated	■ Nervous	■ Uninterested
■ Optimistic	■ Overwhelmed	■ Unmoved
■ Passionate	■ Pessimistic	
■ Respected	■ Responsible	
■ Supported	■ Sad	
■ Validated	■ Skeptical	
	■ Uninformed	
	■ Worried	

Step 4: Post-Consultation Emotional State.

For each issue you listed in step 2, there is a way (or multiple ways) you want the selected DI to feel *after* having a consultation with you. What emotion(s) do you want them to feel *after* the consultation, and why should they now feel that way after meeting with you? Said another way, identify the emotions you want the selected DI to feel after the consultation about each of the issues you address and the reasons why they should now experience those emotions.

Returning to the staffing GM example and the performance issue, how do you want the GM to feel about the staffing issue after your consultation? Perhaps you want them to feel *optimistic* that they have found a provider that can increase their staffing performance.

Use the list of DI emotions in step 3 to identify the ones you want your DI to feel after the consultation.

Step 5: The Emotional Transition.

In the previous two steps, you identified the two end points for the consultation. You now know how the selected DI feels about the issues before the consultation and how you want them to feel after, and you know the reasons for those emotions. During the consultation, an Emotional Transition needs to take place, which is when the deal becomes energized. The salesperson needs to transition the DI's emotions from the ones they felt before to the ones the salesperson wants the DI to feel after the first meeting. There are three Emotional Transition Techniques to use to guide this change:

1. The questions you ask.
2. The information you share visually and verbally.
3. The actions you take before, during, and after the consultation.

These are the three I shared earlier in the chapter that empower you to demonstrate Empathetic Expertise. All of these techniques may or may not be needed to facilitate the transition. That's a determination you need to make based on the circumstance and your Desired Consultation Outcomes. Here are some suggestions when using these tools:

- As you craft questions to transition the DI's emotions, consider asking ones that lead them to think about aspects they had not considered before and those that lead them to think differently about aspects they had already thought about. Using the same manufacturing example, you could ask a question like: "What thought have you given to increasing efficiency by implementing a _____?"

- Do not limit the information you share to the words you say. Two-thirds of the population are visual learners. If you don't also use visuals, you'll fail to engage most people, which means you won't arouse their emotions. Visuals can be pictures, graphs, charts, etc.

- Rather than share information in terms of facts and figures, share stories, as I present in chapter 7.

- Given the nature of the circumstance, actions may also be taken before, during, and/or after the consultation. An example would be an article you send after the consultation regarding an issue you discussed and the ramifications of not addressing it immediately.

- For each technique, be mindful of not just the technique itself but also how you perform it. As I shared with the "Rocky story," it wasn't just the questions the euthanasia service provider asked; it was also their tone that transitioned my emotions.

DI Emotional Transition is complex, and the approach cannot be taken lightly. Plus, the transition is guaranteed to fail if you lack Empathetic Expertise. The best word to describe the needed approach is *surgical*. You need to be precise in how you go about this transition, or it will come across as disingenuous, and you'll have nothing but a tarnished relationship.

Emotional Transition Scenarios

There are eight potential scenarios regarding the need for an Emotional Transition during the first meeting that you may encounter, each requiring a unique strategy given the circumstances. People are commonly motivated by fear and greed. Depending on the individual and the circumstance, one is often more prevalent than the other. You won't always know which is more prevalent, but the more emotions you arouse that guide them to the solution, the more likely a deal comes to fruition.

Below are examples of each of those scenarios and the Emotional Transition needed. The important takeaway is that, regardless of which scenarios apply to your circumstances, you need to plan before the consultation to guide these transitions successfully.

- **Negative to Positive.** This is the most straightforward transition to understand. For example, when meeting with the staffing GM, if the expected emotion before your interaction is "frustrated" (a negative emotion) regarding their staffing performance, the desired emotion after the consultation might be "optimistic" (a positive emotion). The Emotional Transition Techniques may include your asking questions to best understand the DI's challenges associated with staffing performance and sharing information on your approach to improving performance.
- **Positive to Negative.** This is the most delicate of the eight scenarios. If the expected emotion before meeting with the DI is "overconfident" (a positive emotion), and you need to give them a dose of reality, don't be the one to burst their balloon. In other words, don't tell them that they are wrong to be euphoric.

    For example, the staffing GM feels "happy" (a positive emotion) about their performance management, but you know they could improve by implementing your solution. In this case, you would ask questions that expose the possibility of higher performance in a way that leads them to recognize the opportunity without your telling them.

The Emotional Transition Technique to use for this transition is questions. Ask them questions that lead them down the path so they see what you see (i.e., that there are opportunities for improvement), and lead them to an emotion of "concern." If you are the one to deliver bad news, you run the risk of the DI looking for a salesperson who will tell them what they want to hear, and you'll lose the deal.

In this scenario, Emotional Transition is most effective when you guide the DI to see the issue for themselves rather than lecturing them. No one wants to be told what to do when they aren't seeking advice.

■ **Negative to More Negative.** Let's say that before your consultation, a call center manager is "frustrated" (a negative emotion) with the technology they have in place. You determine that this frustration has existed for five years, but they haven't done anything about it. A transition from negative to positive by itself is not likely to create motivating energy because they haven't done anything about the issue despite knowing about it for five years.

The more effective approach is transitioning their emotions from negative to more negative. Using this example, consider the following: Are they losing clients or employees? Is their brand being tarnished? Is the competition getting a leg up on them? All of these questions create fear that can motivate them to take action. Help them see the compounded effect of the issues to finally get them to move out of the status quo. Remember, if you want them to do something, they have to feel something.

The most effective Emotional Transition Technique to accomplish this is asking questions that lead the DI to feel this issue's total impact on the organization and themselves.

- **Positive to More Positive.** This is the easiest transition to guide because you build off their energy. Let's say, for example, the DI is "intrigued" (a positive emotion) about making a change in provider before the consultation. After your consultation, the desired emotion is "excitement" (a positive emotion) about what you offer. All three Emotional Transition Techniques could be needed in this scenario. The pitfall to avoid is overselling. By oversharing information, you could unintentionally create a DI concern. Share just enough to transition the emotion, but don't go overboard.

- **Neutral to Negative.** Sometimes, you will have a DI who is "complacent" (a neutral emotion) on a topic, and you want to arouse a negative set of emotions. A great example of this is FOMO (fear of missing out). If they are complacent on a topic and you help them recognize they are missing out on an opportunity, "fear" (a negative emotion) could drive them to act. Or you know they are overpaying for their current situation, but they are unaware of it. A feeling of "frustration" or "anger" (negative emotions) when they become aware they are unknowingly overpaying can create the emotional energy to explore a change to you.

- **Neutral to Positive.** Consider a situation where your prospecting charisma got you in the door, and the DI agreed to have a consultation with you, but they don't know much about your company and what you offer. Because they are unfamiliar with your offerings, they are likely "complacent" (a neutral emotion) about buying from you. Given that, you would want them to become "intrigued" (a positive emotion) at the end of the consultation after they become aware of what your company offers and how it can benefit them. A great question to ask at the end of the first meeting that exposes the success of the Emotional Transition is: "What is your impression of our company now versus before we met?"

■ **Negative to Neutral.** An example of the need for this transition is a Decision Influencer's fear of change. Change is painful. They love the idea of having your solution rather than what they have today. But they may perceive the work involved to make the change as burdensome, which creates "fear" (a negative emotion) that can become a deal killer. A visual tool that helps with this emotional transition is a documented client onboarding plan that depicts how they go from what they have today to working with you. The tool aims to give the DI confidence that the discomfort and disruption will be minimal and the process will be successful. They won't necessarily be "excited" (a positive emotion) about onboarding, but that process will no longer deter them. You've moved them from a negative emotion to a neutral one. Failure to address their negative emotions could jeopardize the deal.

■ **Positive to Neutral.** Sometimes what you sell lacks a feature the DI wants (or currently has). For the deal to come to fruition, you need to transition their emotions from "liking" what they have (a positive emotion) to "not caring" (a neutral emotion) about that feature because of everything else they get when working with you. This emotional transition likely requires using all three Emotional Transition Techniques: questions you ask, information you share, and actions you take.

Once you have concluded this workshop, you have in your hands one of the most powerful sales tools anyone could give you. In chapter 4, you created a Decision Influencer Analysis, which focused on gathering factual information regarding the issues you address for DIs. In this workshop, you've understood the emotional aspects of the issues you address and developed a plan to engage the DI's emotions to motivate them to act. Wait until you see the impact of this on your consultations and every other step of the sales process. You'll have deeper relationships and engagement at levels you've never experienced before.

Practicing What I Preach

I conduct virtual masterclasses and workshops several times a year with attendees ranging from salespeople to business owners and every role in between. After each event, my business development team contacts the attendees to schedule consultations with me. These thirty-minute sessions focus entirely on the attendees as they learn how to implement the strategies I presented.

Last week, while working on this chapter, I had a consultation with someone from my Empathetic Expertise virtual workshop. About fifteen minutes into the meeting, she asked me how to build a comfortable rapport during a consultation. In response, I asked her a thought-provoking question: "During the fifteen minutes we've been talking, what have I told you about me and what I do?" She paused and said, "Nothing," which was the correct answer. I asked her if she felt we had a comfortable rapport, and she said we did. I asked her, "Why do you think we have a comfortable rapport?" She was silent for a moment, and then the light bulb went off. "Because you researched my background and made this conversation entirely about me." Bingo! That's how you build comfortable rapport.

Let's unpack how that happened. Among the Desired Consultation Outcomes on my list is "Transitioned their emotions to our desired ones." In other words, I need to demonstrate Empathetic Expertise.

After the consultation was scheduled, I had some *preparation* to do if I was to achieve that Outcome. I researched her and her company. While reviewing her LinkedIn profile, I learned she had been in several operations roles with the company for over eighteen years but had been in sales for only about six months. That information set a direction for the conversation as I correctly theorized that she was still trying to find her way in sales. She came into this consultation feeling nervous, unsure, and frustrated about her sales position. My goal was for her to come away from the conversation feeling empowered with the new tools she learned.

My preparation also allowed me to provide her with meaningful value. At the end of the consultation, she was all smiles and talked about how much she had learned that she would implement immediately. Because of this experience, she is introducing my firm to her leadership team, who highly respects her given her tenure, and is recommending my Empathetic Expertise program for their entire sales organization. The consultation ended without me ever talking about myself and what I offer. But because of how I conducted the first meeting, she *felt* strongly that I could help her entire sales organization. That's the power of Empathetic Expertise!

If you are looking for a differentiator to make you stand out in a meaningful way in a competitive selling environment and help you develop deeper relationships with DIs, focus on developing Empathetic Expertise. Use that expertise to transition emotions during consultations, energizing your deals. Logic-based consultations will be pleasant conversations but won't lead you to add new clients to your portfolio.

In the next two chapters, I present strategies that help you energize your deals by engaging emotions through the questions you ask and the information you share.

THE FIRST MEETING DIFFERENTIATOR: CONCEPT #5

Emotion is the deal energizer. Without it, the deal has no life. Salespeople need to transition Decision Influencer emotions from their initial state to the desired ones during the consultation.

CHAPTER 6

DEVELOPING QUESTIONS THAT QUALIFY DEALS, DIFFERENTIATE YOU, AND MAKE YOUR CONSULTATIONS MAGICAL

The questions you ask during a consultation serve several purposes. They help you qualify deals, establish trust, differentiate you and what you sell, demonstrate Empathetic Expertise, determine what information to share, and more. This chapter helps you master the art of query during consultations. Yes, asking questions is an art. How you phrase them, when you ask them, your tone in asking them, and the sequence in which you ask them are all important considerations when developing your consultation strategy. A question asked inappropriately or at the wrong time can destroy rapport or create trust issues during this critical deal foundation step.

However, the consultation becomes almost magical if you ask thoughtful, insightful, comprehensive questions. Such questions make the DI feel they received meaningful value from the first meeting, motivate them to address issues, and feel you genuinely care about them . . . to name just a few Outcomes.

Timing is another aspect that makes asking questions an art. Suppose you are a DI, and my first question is: "How much money is in your wallet?" You would likely have a negative impression of me because I had not yet earned the right to ask such an invasive question. While "understanding the funding source for the initiative" may be on your Desired Consultation Outcomes list, careful consideration is needed to determine the right timing for that question.

Timing also includes the sequence of your questions. When questions are not asked logically, meaning in a conversational order, DIs may find the consultation frustrating, and you won't acquire the information you desire.

As I shared in chapter 2, a DI will tolerate only so many questions during a consultation before they shut down on the salesperson. Question selection is another reason that choosing the Desired Consultation Outcomes is the starting point for effective first meeting strategy development. The only questions to ask during consultations are those that help you achieve your selected Outcomes.

Questions should also be more than just acquiring information. They should also uncover a DI's motivation to address their issues, as Steven Harmon painfully learned in the lesson below.

Dream Deal or Nightmare

Steven Harmon, a salesperson for ABC Enterprises, conducted a consultation with a prospective client, Nicole Jamison. During the first meeting, Nicole talked about issues with their current provider. She shared her frustrations, and, as she did, Steven tried not to drool because this deal looked so good. Given Nicole's pain with her current provider, this was a done deal, right? Or was it?

After the consultation, Steven went home, sat on his deck, and dreamed of how he would spend his fat commission check. *I think I'll finally buy that boat I've always wanted*, Steven thought. He even told his wife of his impending big commission and the boat plan.

The following day, Steven arrived at work, opened his email, and was greeted by this message.

Hi Steven,
Thank you for your time yesterday. After further thought, we
have decided to stay with our current provider. If anything
changes, I'll be back in touch.

—Nicole Jamison

Steven stared at his PC in disbelief for what felt like hours. The email
didn't make sense, given Nicole's issues and that his company offered a
solution to address them. He replayed the meeting repeatedly in his mind,
trying to figure out what went wrong. But he came up empty. And the
boat he had been dreaming of had just sunk.

As you read this story, I'm sure a lost deal (or maybe a few) came to
mind despite your having uncovered issues during the consultation. Like
Steven, you were probably baffled (and maybe still are, even today) as to
why you didn't get the deal. You are about to learn where Steven and so
many salespeople go wrong.

Pain: Reality or Mirage

Steven heard the issues described as "pain." He assumed the Decision
Influencer was prepared to do something about it. His mistake was in
thinking that Nicole was ready to make a change.

PAIN. Has a sales book been written, a course delivered, or a sales
video created that didn't preach the importance of salespeople finding
pain when discussing the DI's issues? They all say: *The key to winning
deals is finding buyer pain.* Salespeople have been given that counsel for
years. During pipeline reviews, sales managers inquire about the pain
their salespeople uncovered to evaluate the strength of deals. Are the sales
pundits wrong about their message to salespeople regarding DI pain? No!
In most cases, their counsel is not wrong, but it is incomplete. And this

causes salespeople to believe they have a real deal in the pipeline when it is nothing more than a sales mirage.

Let's step back and define what DI pain is. Pain is the set of issues a DI is experiencing that impede current performance or prevent future growth. In other words, pain has both negative and positive aspects. For example, if a continually malfunctioning machine prevents achieving current production requirements, that's one form of pain. If an IT manager wants faster performance, but the technology is unable to support that growth objective, that's another type of pain. Pain can be an objective, a roadblock, an obstacle, or even a goal that a DI has. They are considered pain because they hurt both the DI and their employer.

Regardless of which of the two types of pain the DI is experiencing (positive or negative), there is a flaw in most salespeople's consultation strategy, which causes them to erroneously think a deal is more likely to come to fruition than it actually is. The strategic flaw is that salespeople don't dig deep enough to determine whether the pain they heard is an *inconvenience* or a *problem*, which was the flaw in Steven's case. When Nicole talked about the issues, he heard pain. To him, that meant she was ready to address it. But he was wrong in his assessment.

Inconvenience or Problem

Let's define the difference between an *inconvenience* and a *problem*. An *inconvenience* is an annoyance, a nuisance. DIs may talk about the issues and complain about them, but they won't do anything about them until they elevate to the level of a *problem*. Only then will DIs invest the time, resources, and dollars necessary to address the issues. In chapter 5, I talked about the power of emotion and how it energizes deals. If you want them to do something, they need to feel something. Pain, when DIs perceive it as a *problem*, sparks the level of emotion needed for them to make a change.

Every time I drive into my garage, I see a rubber strip lining the garage door that is no longer properly attached. And each time I pull in, I think, "I should fix that." It's been years, and I still have done nothing. If we had a storm and water came into the garage because of the faulty lining, I'd immediately fix it. Right now, it's an *inconvenience*. A flood makes this issue a *problem*. Think about your own circumstances. How many issues do you talk about but never do anything to resolve? I'm sure it's a good-sized list. Nothing on the issues list gets addressed until it reaches the level of a *problem*.

Salespeople love to use the word *solutions* when talking with DIs. They say it all the time. "We sell solutions!" Well, solutions correlate with *problems*, not *inconveniences*. People look to solve *problems*, not *inconveniences*. But issues classified as *inconveniences* or *problems* aren't always going to stay *inconveniences* or *problems*. Time elapsing and circumstances changing can convert issues from *inconveniences* to *problems* and vice versa. A great example is with my adorable pup, Kona.

During COVID, like thousands of other families, we added a puppy to our family. My daughter, Jamie, gets all the credit for finding Kona, an adorable cockapoo. She's sweet, fun, and playful. I wake up every morning with her climbing to the top of my pillow, reaching down, and kissing my nose. There's no better way to start your day than with Kona nose kisses.

She does, however, have one frustrating quirk. Whenever someone walks a dog past our home, she goes berserk! She flies into the dining room, runs around our table, and jumps at the windows, trying to get outside to play with a "new friend."

The three windows in our dining room face the sidewalk and have wood blinds covering them. We *had* three sets of wood blinds but were down to two after a Kona incident. One morning, we didn't open the blinds enough to allow Kona to see outside as well as she wanted. A woman walked by our home with her little dog, and, in her excitement, Kona pawed at the blinds until she could see what she wanted to and, in the process, destroyed one of the blinds.

Since the blinds were badly damaged and the window faced the street, we covered the window with a sheet to maintain our privacy. After that incident, not a week went by where Sharon and I didn't talk about buying new window coverings. Yet neither of us visited a store or went online to search for them. We were in no rush to fix this. Why? There was a pandemic going on. No one was coming to visit our home during COVID. The dining room isn't even part of the main traffic flow of our home, so we don't frequently go in there.

That sheet served as a window covering for over a year. Then something huge happened! Sharon came into my office to tell me her parents were coming to visit. "Paul and Gail are coming to town!" There's no way my in-laws would be visiting my home with a sheet covering the dining room window. I couldn't have that happen. They would take their daughter back and maybe even their grandkids! This issue, in an instant, elevated from an *inconvenience* to a *problem*.

Coming back to Steven's story, if he had sold window coverings and met with me before I learned my in-laws were coming to visit, he would have heard about the Kona incident and thought a deal was imminent. He would have later been disappointed when I didn't buy at that time because I didn't see a need to do so. After all, the issue was merely an *inconvenience*.

The Kona story is a great example of an issue changing from an *inconvenience* to a *problem*. But issues can go the other way as well. Imagine you sell outsourced IT development services. During a consultation, you learn that they need to upgrade their back office systems. This account would be a megadeal for you. The following month, the DI's company acquires a competitor of theirs with more robust back office technology, which is not perfect but better than what they presently have. They no longer feel motivated to address the issue now, especially with everything else that comes with an acquisition. The back office systems have gone from a *problem* to an *inconvenience* because of a change in circumstances.

Take a look at your pipeline reports. I bet some deals have languished in those reports month after month. They have had no forward movement, and you scratch your head because you found pain during consultations. Go back and review your notes from those meetings. Was the pain you heard an *inconvenience* or a *problem*? You may very well find that you tricked yourself into believing these deals were real, which, unfortunately for you, is genuine pain.

Horizontal Versus Vertical Questions

Many sales books tell you what you need to do but not necessarily how to do it, which is a pet peeve of mine. I shared with you the hardship of determining if the pain you've heard is an *inconvenience* or a *problem*, but how do you make that determination? I'll tell you how.

I want you to think of the scariest place you can imagine. Did you come up with one? Take that level of "scary" and multiply it by one hundred. That's how scary the place I'm about to take you to is. No one wants to go here, but we do. Most of us go to this place twice per year. Where is this scary place? The dentist's office!

No one looks forward to their routine dental visit for teeth cleaning and the exam. After the hygienist cleans your teeth, the dentist enters the room armed with a sharp, metal-hooked instrument. I always thought we weren't supposed to put metal in our mouths, but I guess there is an exception for dentists, allowing them to put metal in other people's mouths.

She leans the chair back and shines a bright light into our mouths. Always with a perfect smile, she asks us to "open wide" and prepares to begin the examination.

Here comes the big metal hook. Methodically, she presses it into each tooth to see if it will stick. All the while, we are praying to ourselves, *Please don't stick. Please don't stick.* Then, the unimaginable happens. The hook sticks in the tooth, and the dentist conducts a comprehensive examination to determine the *root* cause of the issue.

What if we apply this dental examination approach to your consultation? In chapter 2, I presented the portfolio of potential Desired

Consultation Outcomes. Several of those Outcomes relate to issues the DI is experiencing (for example, pain), which, of course, most salespeople would select. Several of those Outcomes also relate to a DI's motivation to address issues. Most salespeople ask only surface questions during consultations, metaphorically the dentist's hook pressing into each tooth, to learn a piece of information. But when the hook sticks, rather than conduct a comprehensive analysis of the acquired information, they just move on to the "next tooth." In doing so, they fail to achieve the Desired Outcome, which is to understand the DI's motivation to address issues.

Salespeople don't have the luxury of using a literal hook during consultations. However, they do have two question tools: *Horizontal* and *Vertical Questions*. *Horizontal Questions* help you acquire information and learn "the what." These questions are conversation starters regarding a topic. An example of a *Horizontal* question is: What is the biggest challenge you are facing in your business today? The DI answers, and the salesperson writes it down. Too many salespeople immediately move on to their next topical *Horizontal Question* rather than ask *Vertical Questions*.

Vertical Questions expose "the why" behind "the what." These questions uncover the DI's motivation to address the issues. They complete the picture of the information nugget the DI shared. This question type also allows you to demonstrate Empathetic Expertise because asking questions can convey genuine interest in the DI and their issues.

Based on the *Horizontal Question* that was asked regarding the DI's business challenges, appropriate *Vertical Questions* to be asked in follow-up include the following:

- How long has that been an issue?
- How does that issue impact the business?
- What makes this issue the biggest one impacting your business?
- Which departments does this issue affect?
- What is the financial impact of this issue?
- What has been done to address this issue?

- What other methods have been considered to address this issue?
- What were the results of prior efforts to address this issue?
- How important is it to the business to resolve this issue?
- How important is it to you personally to resolve this issue?

It's impossible to provide a complete list of *Vertical Questions* because of the infinite circumstances that may be encountered. Besides, *Vertical Questions* aren't a list of questions. They are a mindset. They are your never-ending quest to develop a comprehensive understanding of a DI's circumstances when they share information with you. In other words, you need to be *Insatiably Inquisitive* because that is the key to determining their level of motivation to address an issue. *Vertical Questions* help you determine if the pain you heard is an *inconvenience* or a *problem*. Salespeople who don't ask enough *Vertical Questions* are the ones who, unfortunately, believe their sales pipelines are stronger than they actually are.

I've developed the following acronym to help you remember the two types of pain and the importance of determining which one the DI is experiencing.

P   =   *Problem*

A   =   *Action*

I   =   *Inconvenience*

N   =   *Neutral*

When DIs perceive pain as a problem, they do something about it.

When pain is merely an inconvenience, DIs remain neutral and do nothing about it.

I can't emphasize enough the importance of *Vertical Questions* and their impact on your ability to qualify deals, demonstrate Empathetic Expertise, and differentiate yourself.

Missed Opportunities

As discussed, *Horizontal Questions* help you acquire information. Two types of Horizontal Questions need to be asked during consultations: *Challenge* and *Positioning*.

By using *Challenge Horizontal Questions*, you can expose aspects DIs perceive could be better or different from what they presently have. However, limiting consultations to what DIs perceive can be better or different than what they have today is flawed. The reason comes back to the question I shared in chapter 1:

> **Who knows more about the world of potential solutions in your industry: you or the people you sell to?**

Every salesperson agrees they know more about the world of potential solutions in their industry than those they sell to. That means the consultation cannot be limited to a Decision Influencer's perceptions. Remember, they don't know what you know. If you limit the consultation to their perceptions, you are missing out on a ton of deals you could have won! Consider the following scenario: What if you, because of your expertise, recognize the DI's issue as a *problem*, but they perceive it as an *inconvenience?* What do you do?

The Injury

On December 31, 2017, I was training in the gym, preparing for the Minnesota State Bench Press Tournament, to be held a few months later. I felt strong that day and was on track to set a new state record at the tournament. Then, without warning: *POP!* It felt like a giant rubber band snapped in my left elbow. I quickly put the weights down and walked over to the mirror. There was immediate swelling in my elbow, about the size of a golf ball. While I had never had this type of injury before, I somehow knew what I had done. I had ruptured my left triceps.

I packed my gear, drove to the sports orthopedics emergency room, and called Sharon, asking her to meet me there. Since this was New Year's Eve day, the ER services were limited. They took an X-ray, but this type of injury does not show in an X-ray. And, due to the holiday, it was not possible to have an MRI. Since there was nothing else they could do for me that day, they sent me home with some pain medication and a sling.

Interestingly, the moment I felt the pop, the pain was brutal. It felt like my arm was crumbling. However, the pain subsided within an hour, even before I took the pain medicine. Something was seriously wrong with my arm, but the pain had become tolerable. I even went out on New Year's Eve with my family.

No imaging facilities were open on New Year's Day, so I still couldn't have an MRI. On January 2, I flew out to deliver a three-day Sales Differentiation® strategy development program to a client. While there, my left arm turned purple from my shoulder to my fingertips. Though my arm turned colors, it still wasn't painful, just uncomfortable and weak.

Despite my injury and the discoloration, the program was tremendously successful. Sitting at the airport gate waiting for my flight home, I thought about what would come next. Obviously, I needed an MRI. If I was right about the issue with my arm, I'd need surgery. Since I wasn't in pain, there seemed to be no reason to rush the surgery. I looked at my calendar, which was full of speaking gigs, group workshops, and consulting engagements. There was a window of time at the end of February that I thought should work to have this medical procedure. That was my plan, or so I thought.

I returned from the trip and had an MRI. Two days later, I had a doctor's consultation to review the results. He entered the examination room with a somber look on his face. He looked me square in the eye and said, "Lee, you have completely ruptured your triceps, and we need to schedule you for surgery."

"I'm not surprised," I said. "What is your availability for the surgery at the end of February?"

He responded, "I'll see you on Monday."

"Which Monday?" I curiously asked.

"This Monday," the doctor quickly responded.

"That doesn't work for me," I countered. "I have a full schedule of client engagements for the next six weeks. Let's look at the end of February."

The doctor leaned back in his chair. "Lee, would you like to be able to use your left arm again? Because here is what you do not realize. I know you are not in a lot of pain right now, but your left triceps are balled up near the top of your shoulder. We have a small window of time to reattach it at the elbow, and the clock is ticking."

My jaw hit the floor. I had no idea there was such an urgency to address this issue. I perceived this issue as an *inconvenience*, but the doctor educated me and helped me realize that this was a *problem* that had to be addressed now. Because I trusted him and knew he had expertise in this field, I immediately changed my perspective and was in the operating room that Monday.

What if, because the doctor didn't want to have a conflict with me, he gave in and said we could do the surgery at the end of February? Of course, the surgical procedure would have been a failure. In the medical field, he would have been guilty of medical malpractice. Why? Because of his specialized expertise, he has an obligation to his patients to help them make informed decisions.

The Disconnect

Like the doctor, salespeople are obligated to help DIs make informed decisions. While the consequences of salespeople failing to educate and inform DIs may not be as dire as those in the medical field, neglecting to do so can have serious consequences for a DI. There will be times during consultations when you ask a *Challenge Horizontal Question* that exposes an issue that the DI perceives as an *inconvenience,* meaning they see it as a nuisance that does not need to be addressed now. But, based on your expertise, you know it's a *problem* they need to address immediately. When that happens, you are at a deal crossroads.

One option is to end that discussion and move on to something else. Salespeople often choose this option because they are afraid of irritating the DI. They worry that trying to continue a conversation regarding this topic to lead the DI to see the issue as a *problem* will anger the DI. They also fear that, by trying to continue the discussion, the DI will perceive them as another one of those pushy salespeople who don't listen.

However, as a sales professional, your earned title, your responsibility is to help your clientele, given your specialized expertise. That expertise is to be used to guide DIs accurately to perceive the issue they feel is an *inconvenience* but that you know is a *problem.* Failure to have that conversation is sales malpractice.

I mentioned that a primary reason salespeople stop the conversation is fear of irritating the DI. Another reason they don't continue the discussion is that they don't know how to do it appropriately in a manner that will comes across as helpful to the DI rather than irritating and pushy.

Those who try to continue the conversation often go into "tell" mode, which is why DIs get irritated. Let's lecture them and tell them they are wrong—that's a surefire way to anger the DI and bring a fast end to the consultation. While a doctor can usually get away with it, salespeople cannot.

As salespeople, we know that we are more knowledgeable about the world of potential solutions in our industry than the DI. However, not all DIs will agree with that assessment. That's especially true if you haven't yet demonstrated specialized expertise, which means you haven't earned the right to counsel the DI. Many DIs feel they know as much about potential solutions as you, maybe even more. (I hope that is never a true statement about you.)

Leading the Witness

Since we know salespeople shouldn't lecture, how should they guide DIs to recognize an issue as a *problem*, not an *inconvenience?* Ask questions! But not just any questions. These questions must be carefully crafted, insightful questions that lead the DI down a path so they see what the salesperson sees.

In a courtroom, litigation attorneys have the expertise to ask witnesses questions in a particular fashion. Their questions paint a picture for the decision-making group, the jury, so they see exactly what the attorney wants them to see. You have the same opportunity with your DIs. Ask questions that paint the picture they need to see. Coming back to my medical episode, when the doctor asked if I wanted to be able to use my left arm again, that certainly made me think and changed my perception of this issue. Something had to be done now.

Earlier, I shared two types of *Horizontal Questions*: *Challenge* and *Positioning*. Resolving this perception disconnect necessitates the use of *Positioning Horizontal Questions*. *Positioning Horizontal Questions* are crafted to lead a DI to think differently about their situation and the solutions they have or could have. Whenever you lead a DI to think differently, you convey specialized expertise, which means you have provided meaningful value. As with *Challenge Horizontal Questions*, *Positioning Horizontal Questions* are conversation starters for a topic that provide you with information but require you to follow up with *Vertical Questions* to be comprehensive.

What both *Challenge Horizontal* and *Positioning Horizontal Questions* have in common is that they

- are used to initiate a conversation regarding a topic,
- are asked in an open-ended fashion (cannot be answered with a yes or no response), and
- require the use of *Vertical Questions* once the door has been opened.

The core difference between them is as follows:

Challenge Horizontal Questions expose aspects DIs <u>perceive</u> could be better or different from what they presently have.

Example: "What is something you'd like to have that your current supplier doesn't provide today?" This question exposes aspects the DI perceives could be better or different from what they currently have.

Positioning Horizontal Questions expose aspects that DIs either <u>don't recognize</u> could be better or different from what they have today, or the issues the DIs perceive as an *inconvenience* that you know is a *problem*.

Example: One of your differentiators relates to inventory management. You might ask, "How does your current supplier handle inventory management for you?" This is a *Positioning Horizontal Question* because you know they aren't currently receiving that service; it is a differentiator of yours, which opens the door to a conversation about it. A *Challenge Horizontal Question* would not expose this opportunity because the DI doesn't know inventory management services are available.

Let's say, for example, you sell air filters to companies. As part of the consultation, you ask, "How do you order air filters?" Is that a *Challenge* or *Positioning Horizontal Question*? The answer is: It depends on why you are asking it.

If you know that DIs commonly perceive ordering as an issue, it's a *Challenge Horizontal Question*. But if you have ordering capabilities your competitors do not have, this is a *Positioning Horizontal Question* intended to open the door to a conversation regarding that differentiator.

Positioning Horizontal Questions are especially important to start a conversation about your differentiator. If you jump on the lecture box and preach about the greatness of your differentiator, the DI will ignore your message because you have not engaged them yet. But when you pique a DI's interest using a *Positioning Horizontal Question*, they will want to hear what you have to say. If developing *Positioning Questions* intrigues you, I encourage you to read *Sales Differentiation*, in which I delve deeply into that concept.

A consultation limited to just DI perceptions of issues is a deal likely to be lost for several reasons. First, you will probably not have differentiated yourself to a level to spark interest in change. Second, the DI probably did not receive much meaningful value during the first meeting because the DI didn't learn anything new. Third, you will not have effectively positioned your company's differentiators. Last, and most importantly, the deal will likely stall because the DI will not be motivated to act as their emotions will not have been aroused. A successful consultation requires using both *Horizontal Question* types as well as *Vertical Questions* to be thorough and energize the deal.

I mentioned earlier that a salesperson has an obligation to guide their DIs to recognize when they have misperceptions regarding an issue. This obligation creates opportunity. If you lead the DI to see the prudence of addressing this issue now because it is a *problem*, you build trust, arouse their emotions, and establish credibility.

You become seen as a valued resource, a trusted adviser with Empathetic Expertise. DIs don't want order takers. If they did, they would buy online instead of talking with you. Plus, leading DIs to recognize issues as *problems*, not *inconveniences*, builds a strong pipeline of solid deals.

Common Art of Query Missteps

As mentioned, asking questions is an art that takes practice to master. Here are some common questioning mistakes salespeople make.

- **Asking too many questions.** There are only so many questions a DI will tolerate before the consultation feels like an interrogation. Effective consultations feel conversational. An important consultation preparation step is to identify where you can consolidate "smaller" questions into larger "meaty ones."

  A technique that reduces the need to ask multiple questions and encourages the DI to share information is called an Overview Question with Cues. An example of this questioning technique is *"Can you share an overview with me of your manufacturing process and touch upon how you handle inventory, compliance, and quality assurance?"*

  While on the surface this appears to be a closed-ended question that chokes conversations, it's not. It's a powerful conversation starter. The DI will respond affirmatively and share that information with you.

  Here's where the magic happens. Those three cues—in this case: inventory, compliance, and quality assurance—are specifically selected to guide the conversation toward the most important topics you want them to cover, which will get them talking for a good five minutes and eliminates the need for you to ask separate questions for each information nugget. Their answer gives you an initial snapshot of their Current Circumstance, but you'll need to ask *Vertical Questions* to develop the complete picture.

  Another way to avoid asking too many questions is to stay focused on your Desired Consultation Outcomes and ask only questions that help you achieve those.

- **Asking too few questions.** Countless studies have revealed that a key to winning deals is salespeople asking thoughtful, insightful, comprehensive questions. While most salespeople ask an appropriate number of *Horizontal Questions*, particularly *Challenge Horizontal Questions*, they don't ask enough *Vertical Questions* to develop a complete picture of the DI's situation. Therefore, they can't create a high enough level of emotion so the DI will be ready to address the issues.

- **Asking too many yes/no questions.** Yes/no questions (aka close-ended questions) choke conversations and create an uncomfortable experience for the DI. When planning your question strategy, look for every opportunity to develop non-yes/no questions (aka open-ended questions) that encourage DIs to openly and comfortably share information with you.

- **Asking the same questions as other salespeople.** One of your goals should be for DIs, at some point during the first meeting, to say, "No one has ever asked me that question." *Boom!* You've made them think, which also means you are providing meaningful value. Asking *Positioning Horizontal Questions* is a great way to differentiate yourself because the competition isn't likely to be asking them.

- **The use of "why" questions.** As mentioned earlier, the purpose of *Vertical Questions* is to develop a complete picture of "the why" behind the information the DI shared. That doesn't mean you should ask a barrage of "why" questions because such questions can create negative feelings.

  Remember when you were a kid and your mom asked, "Why did you do that?" You quaked in your boots and hoped to come up with a satisfactory response. Being asked "why" usually arouses a negative emotion and a feeling of being put on the spot.

  Rather than ask: "Why is it done that way?"

Ask: "How did you and your team develop that approach?"

The answer to either question provides the information you need, but the latter does not create a negative feeling.

On the other hand, questions starting with *why* can spur action. Imagine asking a why question of a newly hired CIO, such as, "Why do you do it this way?" She has no ownership of the current process, and that question may lead her to dig into those reasons, which can energize your deal. But asking that question of a tenured CIO can make them feel defensive and harm your relationship with them.

- **Only asking "perception" questions.** This point was addressed when describing the purpose of *Challenge Horizontal* and *Positioning Horizontal Questions*. Relying exclusively on what a DI perceives can be better or different than what they have today is a deal-risking proposition. Remember, you know more than they do about the world of potential solutions in your industry, which exposes opportunities to differentiate what and how you sell by asking *Positioning Horizontal Questions*.

- **Asking confusing questions.** If a DI says, "I don't understand your question," you've likely created an uncomfortable moment. This often happens when salespeople use jargon familiar to them but not to their DIs. As you develop questions, ensure they are phrased so that your DI will understand what you are asking of them.

There may be occasions, however, when you intentionally want the "I don't understand your question" response because it allows you to expand upon the issue you are trying to high-light. For example, you ask, "What are the internal costs for that service?" The DI responds, "I don't understand what you mean." Now the door is open for you to say, "Many clients have not evaluated the issue from the perspective of internal costs. We have found that this issue has recruiting, hardware, and management cost implications. What have you found in your organization?" In this case, by design, the question comes back to the salesperson for clarification. But if that is not your intent, the consultation becomes awkward if the DI doesn't understand what you are asking.

- **Asking nonsequential questions.** When asking questions of a DI, you put their brain to work. To receive the most helpful information, ask questions sequentially. If you do, they will share more information because they can build upon their prior responses. When questions are asked out of sequence, you'll disrupt the DI's thought process and may confuse them. If they get confused, they get frustrated, which spoils the consultation experience. When planning your questions, sequence them logically so the DI can follow and give you the level of information you desire in a conversational format.

In chapter 2, I presented three categories of Desired Consultation Outcomes: Current Circumstance, Future Solution, and Decision Framework. Those categories give you a way to sequentially ask questions and give the consultation a logical, easy-to-follow flow.

Asking Current Circumstance questions leads to your understanding of the current situation, how it is being provided, who is providing it, and how satisfied they are with how it is being provided.

Asking Future Solution questions lead to you understanding their intended direction for the relationship, including: objectives, scope, requirements, and competition.

Asking Decision Framework questions lead to you understanding how their decision will be made, including: the decision-making group, decision-making process, price considerations, and contract considerations.

The questions within those three categories are *Challenge Horizontal* and *Positioning Horizontal Questions* as well as *Vertical Questions*.

- **Asking invasive questions before earning the right to do so.** This chapter opened with me asking, "How much money is in your wallet?" That's an invasive question. Effective consultations include questions ranging from least to most invasive. As the salesperson earns credibility and trust, the DI will become more comfortable with sensitive questions. When planning your consultation strategy, rank your questions from least to most invasive and sequence them so that the most invasive ones are asked only when you've earned the right to do so.

When you began this chapter, if you doubted my use of the word *art* to describe a consultation's questioning strategy, I hope you've come away with a different perspective. Which questions are asked, how they are asked, and when they are asked significantly affect the success of the first meeting.

Download my favorite consultation questions at www.LeesQuestions .com.

Once you've acquired the information you need during the consultation and can begin "diagnosing" the opportunity, it's your turn to share information. The question is how to do so effectively, which you'll learn in the next chapter.

THE FIRST MEETING DIFFERENTIATOR: CONCEPT #6

The art of query helps salespeople understand a Decision Influencer's issues, qualify deals, expose opportunities, arouse emotions, and understand the level of interest in addressing those issues.

CHAPTER 7

FEATURES, BENEFITS, AND BOREDOM

HOW TO SHARE COMPELLING STORIES THAT ENGAGE, EXCITE, AND DIFFERENTIATE

A fter completing the information acquisition component of the consultation and achieving the related Desired Consultation Outcomes, the next step is to share relevant information with the Decision Influencer to motivate them to address issues and move the relationship forward. Consultations often go awry at this stage for several reasons:

- Too much irrelevant information is shared, which causes Decision Influencer disinterest and creates trust issues.
- Unbelievable superlatives are tossed out without proof, leading to trust concerns (e.g., "We are the best provider!").
- Information is presented in terms of features and benefits, which may not appear problematic, but it is, as I explain later in the chapter.
- Information is shared in a hard-to-understand fashion, which confuses the DI and leads to frustration and irritation.

- Salespeople not being mindful of their nonverbal messages and not paying attention to their DI's nonverbal responses.

Remember why DIs agree to consultations: to become wiser about the issues they are experiencing and to understand the potential remedies. Keeping that in the forefront of your mind serves as a guide to the information-sharing component of the consultation.

Too Much Irrelevant Information Shared

When it comes to sharing information during consultations, don't share too much information, or too little. Share the right amount to achieve the Desired Consultation Outcomes you selected. Remember the overarching objective of the consultation:

> Pique a high enough level of interest with Decision Influencers so that they want to continue interacting with you after the consultation.

How do you determine the right amount of information to share? Many salespeople ask themselves, What do I want to tell the Decision Influencer?

That approach leads to several issues. The salesperson

- talks way too much during the consultation,
- runs out of time and doesn't convey the most important, relevant information, and
- fails to foster engagement with the DI or transition their emotions.

Consider the potential information to share like a massive database with terabytes of data. The question, *What do I want to tell the DI?* does not serve as an adequate "search engine" to find the information to convey during the consultation. Candidly, it's a poor question for salespeople to use for their information-sharing strategy because it places all the emphasis on themselves rather than on the DI, bringing us back to the perils of having a discovery mindset.

Effective information sharing during consultations necessitates skipping that question and instead asking two foundational introspective questions. The first is as follows:

What do I want them to remember?

This question is a game changer when it comes to information sharing. Now the focus is entirely on the DI and the information they will retain.

When the focus is on remembering, we also need to be mindful of Hermann Ebbinghaus and the Forgetting Curve. In the late 1800s, Ebbinghaus conducted a learning and memory study that led to the creation of the Forgetting Curve. This analysis revealed the decline of memory retention over time, and the results, still considered valid today, were staggering.

Ebbinghaus found that people forget 50 percent of what they learn within twenty-four hours and remember about 10 percent of that information a week later. Applying that model to a consultation, the DI remembers about six minutes of a sixty-minute meeting. Just six minutes!

You may want to tell them everything about what you offer, but they won't remember it all, only a tiny fraction. So salespeople need to be mindful of the information they share and how they share it. The good news is you don't need to tell them everything during the first meeting. You need to tell them the *right things*, which are a function of your Desired Consultation Outcomes. Based on what you learned from your questions (and beforehand, during your planning), the DI needs to hear the most relevant information about their circumstance so they desire additional interactions with you.

I highly suggest reading the prior paragraph again. It sets a very important tone for information sharing and is a key component of a successful consultation.

The second foundational introspective question is as follows:

> **For the DI to feel this consultation was a great use of their time, what information do they want to learn?**

Most salespeople never consider the first meeting from this perspective because they have a discovery mindset. As I discussed in chapter 1, salespeople often focus solely on what they want to accomplish and are not mindful of what would be of value to the DI. This lack of consideration leads to DIs coming away from the consultation experience disappointed and likely uninterested in more interactions with the salesperson, making the first meeting a failure.

How can salespeople determine what information to share during the consultation? For starters, ask your DI! So much of selling is an open-book test, and many salespeople fail to recognize that. Once you procure the consultation, say something like this:

> **"When we get together, I plan to share some recent industry insights, trends, and best practices you should be aware of, and where we fit within those. Is there any other information you want me to be prepared to share with you while we are together?"**

If you aren't already asking that question, try it. You'll be amazed by what DIs tell you they want to learn when they meet with you that you aren't currently sharing.

In addition to asking the DI for that information, three questions will be on their mind. These questions are on their minds regardless of what you sell, to what industry you sell, and the level of the person you conduct a consultation with. Whether they tell you or not, these are the three questions DIs expect you to address during the consultation:

1. Why change what we are doing?
2. Why change now?
3. Why change to you?

The information you share must clearly answer those questions to keep your deal moving forward and for your DI to desire future interactions with you. If any of those questions are not answered in an easy-to-understand manner, expect the status quo to take this deal away from you.

Earlier, I talked about sharing the right amount of information. But what is the right amount? A helpful concept is "The Rule of Three." Multiple studies have revealed that people tend to learn and remember information in terms of themes, or clusters of information, put into three distinct categories. As you plan your consultations, consider three primary themes you want the DI to remember. My recommendation is to focus on three differentiators you want to stick in their minds. When sharing information, always share it in the context of those three themes (differentiators).

Here's the test that indicates if your information-sharing approach worked. Imagine the meeting is over, and someone asks them what they learned during the consultation. Success has been achieved when the DI can cite those three themes.

Unbelievable Superlatives

"Our product is the *best* in the industry." As you read that sentence, you probably visualized a salesperson with a huge smile and chest puffed out as they share this information nugget. By saying this, the salesperson thinks they are achieving two consultation Outcomes: building relationships and differentiating themselves from the competition. Unfortunately, they are wrong on both counts.

When salespeople use unbelievable superlatives like "best" with no evidence, rather than build relationships, they turn people off. DIs think: "According to whom? And based on what metrics?" Those unsupported expressions result in the infamous "buyer eye roll." You may not always see it, but it's there. While a crucial goal is for salespeople to build a bond with the DI, these expressions do precisely the opposite. They reduce the DI's interest in working with you because they won't believe these unsubstantiated claims, and trust will be damaged.

When salespeople use unbelievable, unsupported superlatives to differentiate themselves from the competition, they achieve the exact opposite: They come across like every other salesperson, which means they commoditize themselves.

Unless you can prove it, don't say it! How many salespeople tell prospects the following? "Our people are pretty good. Our service is okay. Our technology is eh." None of them. Every salesperson boasts of having the best people, service, and technology. But unless you can prove those to be true, the message is a DI turnoff rather than a turn-on.

An alternative approach that builds trust is to say this:

> **I'll share with you what our clients say makes us different and that they find beneficial.**

That sentence conveys an entirely different message than you unilaterally claiming to be the best.

Some superlatives are true and potentially believable, like being "the biggest." The common mistake is failing to provide context when sharing the differentiator. So what, you're the biggest? Why should the DI care? What value do they get from your being the biggest? Also, some DIs may see being the biggest as a negative rather than a positive.

When it comes to differentiators, if you don't give them context, one of two bad things happens:

1. The DI never figures out why the differentiator matters to them.
2. The DI gives the differentiator a meaning that is not helpful to your deal.

It has much more of an impact when a salesperson says, "We are the largest provider in the industry, which gives us the most buying power, allowing us to reduce costs for our clients." That is a message point that will be embraced and remembered while helping you stand out from the competition.

Constructing Compelling Stories

Since the beginning of sales time, a core concept has been preached to salespeople, "You have to present features with benefits." Most salespeople have interpreted that expression literally, so when they share information, they robotically rattle off features and benefits. (Some still just share features, which is another issue entirely.) As many have discovered, that approach usually comes across as boring, creates little engagement, and fails to arouse emotions. As I discussed in chapter 5, emotion is the deal energizer. Without it, the deal is flat and likely to stall out.

So, if salespeople aren't to use features and benefits, how can they effectively communicate what they offer? Stories! Everyone enjoys a well-told story. Think back to your childhood. Nothing was better than your day ending with a story told by your mom or dad. People embrace stories regardless of their age or job title. Learning is much more effective when information is shared in a story format since storytelling helps with retention, which is obviously one of the goals when sharing them. People remember stories more than facts. But they remember the facts enveloped in stories.

Here's the key for salespeople to leverage storytelling. They need a portfolio of stories they can pull from as different selling situations arise. Unfortunately, most companies don't have what I call a Deal Pursuit Story Portfolio, leaving salespeople with no choice other than rattling off features and benefits. While veteran salespeople may have picked up on a handful of stories shared by others during other deal pursuits, what about the rest of the stories? And what about newly hired salespeople? How will they learn these stories? Without that Portfolio, they won't, and that's a sales organization's weakness.

If you are a sales leader reading this book, my recommendation is to create a Deal Pursuit Story Portfolio. It should address every solution you offer so your salespeople can select stories from it to share when preparing for consultations. Even better, include stories for each prospect circumstance (for example, using a specific competitor of yours, outsourcing for the first time, having a particular issue, etc.), industry, and company size you serve relative to the solutions offered. Of course, in a perfect world, you would have stories for every solution and every market segment. Most likely, you don't, and I'll come back to how to handle those situations. For each solution for which you lack a story, create one for the Target Client Profile (see chapter 3) of that solution.

Start the process of developing your Portfolio by setting a goal this week of creating three stories addressing the top challenges your salespeople face. This begins your Portfolio development journey. Commit to doing this exercise weekly until the Portfolio is entirely constructed.

Once the Portfolio is constructed, the magic comes when you bring the stories to life. Have practice sessions where the salespeople present the stories to their peers. Create storytelling contests (salespeople love contests!) and award prizes for the most effective ones from your Portfolio.

If you are a salesperson intrigued by the concept of sharing information through storytelling, but the company hasn't developed a Deal Pursuit Story Portfolio, create your own. Interview colleagues and management to learn the background of deals that have been won.

Within the Portfolio, structure existing client stories with these components:

1. *Their Circumstances.* This addresses size, industry, and any other circumstances that would be helpful for your salespeople to know.
2. *Their Objectives.* The goals, concerns, challenges, and priorities that needed to be addressed for them to become a client of yours.
3. *Their Pre-Solution Emotions.* How the DI felt about the objectives and why they felt that way. (See chapter 5.)
4. *Your Solution.* What was implemented to achieve the client's objectives.
5. *Their Results.* Cite both the tangible and intangible results. Tangible results are data. Intangible results include anecdotal feedback like "Our users are much happier with the new solution."
6. *Their Post-Solution Emotions.* How the DI feels about your solution and results, and why they now feel that way.

The Portfolio provides the building blocks to construct compelling stories. Unlike your childhood ones that focused on enjoyment, these stories need to convey a strong message point (or points) that will be remembered.

Here is an example of what would be included as a client entry in a Deal Pursuit Story Portfolio.

1. *Their Circumstances.* Large hospitality company.
2. *Their Objectives.* Reduce shipping costs.
3. *Their Pre-Solution Emotions.* Unhappy with how much they were paying for shipping and frustrated because they had not been able to figure out a way to reduce these costs with their current provider.
4. *Your Solution.* Your Cost Management Wizard.
5. *Their Results.* Reduced shipping costs by 19 percent within six months.
6. *Their Post-Solution Emotions.* Thrilled with the results because they did not think it was possible and loves our Cost Management Wizard because it is easy to use.

Based on the data points provided in the Portfolio, a salesperson can deliver a story like this:

> **What you shared with me today reminds me of a large hospitality client of ours. They are similar in size to your company and were unhappy with how much they were spending on shipping and couldn't find a way to reduce this expenditure with their current provider. They had tried everything they could think of and were frustrated because they couldn't get those costs down. They implemented our Cost Management Wizard, which creatively reduces shipping costs, and six months later, their shipping costs were reduced by 19 percent. They are thrilled because they didn't think it was possible to reduce costs, and they love our Wizard because it is so easy to use!**

When sharing the story, you'll notice the aroused emotion by using words such as *unhappy*, *frustrated*, and *thrilled*. As I've shared a few times, emotion is the deal energizer. The stories can't just be factual. They need to be compelling and arouse emotion. The goal is for your DI to feel something that causes them to act after hearing the story: If you want them to do something, they need to feel something.

Let's raise the bar and make the prior story even more compelling. Let's present the information in this fashion.

> **What you shared with me today reminds me of a large hospitality client of ours, like you. We were able to reduce their shipping costs by 19 percent. They too were unhappy with how much they were spending on shipping and couldn't reduce this expenditure with their current provider. They had tried everything they could think of and were frustrated because they couldn't get those costs down. They implemented our Cost Management Wizard, which creatively reduces shipping costs, and six months later, their shipping costs were reduced by 19 percent. They are thrilled and love our Wizard because it is so easy to use!**

In this example, the salesperson twice mentioned the 19-percent cost reduction. That was not accidental. It was intentional. When thinking about what they wanted the DI to remember, the savings were a point they wanted to stick in their DI's mind.

The difference between the two messaging approaches is content structure. The first version told the story sequentially: *Their Objectives, Your Solution, and Their Results*. The second approach used a nonsequential format of *The Results, Their Objectives, and Your Solution*. Both storytelling approaches are effective. But I prefer the latter because of the emphasis on results, which is what people buy.

As mentioned, you may not have a client success story for every circumstance. Here is a story constructed when you don't have a client success story to serve as an example but instead uses the information from your Target Client Profile.

What you shared with me today is exactly why we created our Cost Management Wizard for hospitality companies. So often, we hear from executives like you that they are unhappy with how much they spend on shipping and cannot reduce this expenditure with their current provider. They have tried everything they could think of to reduce shipping costs and were frustrated because they couldn't get those costs down. Our Cost Management Wizard creatively reduces shipping costs with a savings expectation of as much as 19 percent. Clients give us great feedback on our Wizard because it is so easy to use. They love it.

When You Don't Have a Direct Client Story

Sometimes, salespeople need stories to effectively position differentiators that don't have a direct client tie-in like the earlier examples. In this case, contrasts to other industries can be used to make concepts easily understandable for your Decision Influencers.

Here's an example of the need for that. I've worked with several clients that structure their pricing as all-inclusive packages. Their clients love the model because it makes it easy for them to budget. However, this model can make their fees appear grossly higher than those of competitors that use an à la carte pricing approach.

With those clients, we collaborated to create an easily relatable and understandable story regarding the pricing model: purchasing an airline ticket. Some airlines, like Delta, provide all-inclusive pricing. Some, like Frontier, use à la carte pricing. On the surface, Frontier usually looks much cheaper than Delta. But when you peel back the layers and analyze Frontier's ticket, you find they charge for seat selection, flight changes, carry-on luggage, and beverages and snacks. Delta's ticket includes all of those. When you compare Frontier's total cost to Delta's, you will see that their pricing is usually very similar.

If you sell using all-inclusive pricing and your competitors sell using à la carte pricing, this is a great story to share because most people have bought airline tickets and can relate. Taking it a step further, if most players in your space offer à la carte pricing, don't wait for the price to become an issue. Proactively share this story so they won't get sticker shock.

I can't emphasize enough the importance of having a Deal Pursuit Story Portfolio. It will pay immediate dividends with both your existing and newly hired salespeople.

Messaging Tools

Read the two statements below. They seem to contradict one another, but they support one another as you share information with Decision Influencers.

> **Two-thirds of people are visual learners. People cannot read and listen at the same time.**

Let's talk through the first statement. When talking about your company and what you offer, if you share information only verbally, two-thirds of DIs won't embrace your message because they don't absorb information that way. They need to see something: a visual. The question to be asked is: What visual will most effectively reinforce what you're sharing verbally? The expression "A picture is worth a thousand words" rings true in this case.

When someone contracts with me to deliver a keynote, in advance of the talk, the host sometimes asks if they can have a copy of my slide deck. They are accustomed to internally developed slides chock-full of text, which make them useful as stand-alone tools. I explain that a professional keynote speaker's slide deck is meaningless without their talk accompanying it. This point turns the conversation toward recording the event rather than sharing my slides. My slides reinforce the points I'm making and have no value by themselves. The same should hold true with your consultation visuals.

If your visual tools are complex or have a lot of text, Decision Influencers will focus on trying to understand them or will be reading the text rather than listening to what you are saying. Try reading while listening to someone talk. You can't do it. Have you ever tried talking with someone who's reading a text message? They don't hear you, do they? People either focus on the visual or the spoken word. You need to pick one.

Nilli Lavie, a psychology and brain science professor at University College London, conducted a study in 2015 that revealed that "hearing and vision tap the same brain regions." In an article published on Today .com, Lavie said, "The more taxing the visual task, the less likely the person is going to hear what you are saying. The reason we can't multitask hearing and vision is these two senses share access to a part of the brain, the association cortex, whose job it is to integrate all incoming information."

This study tells salespeople that they need to be more mindful of the visuals they use than they are today. Too much text or visual complexity leads to the DI turning off their ears and focusing exclusively on the visual.

This "audio-visual" issue affects not just consultations but sales presentations too. Often, the slides have either complex graphics or too much text on them. Rather than reinforcing the spoken word, the slides become a distraction and reduce messaging effectiveness.

The "audio-visual" issue arises because companies attempt to use one tool for two purposes, and it doesn't work. It is common practice to use the visual for both message reinforcement during the consultation and as a leave-behind document. If the visual has so much information that no explanation is needed, that's a red flag. It's not the right tool for consultations because it will detract from the conversation.

What's the solution? Salespeople need two types of messaging tools to support their consultations. The first is for use during consultations. This visual should have very few words on it and be easy for a DI to understand and digest. It should draw the eye to a word, a phrase, a data point, a graphic, or a photo. The sole purpose of this tool is to reinforce the spoken word during the meeting.

The other messaging tool is the leave-behind document. Whether that be print or digital, it includes a narrative explanation of what you offer. When someone reads this document, the goal is to get an agreeing head nod as the DIs read the same message they heard during the consultation. Obviously, the salesperson won't see the nodding because they won't be in the room, but this is what happens when the consultation and the messaging tools are properly designed and aligned.

If the "one tool for two purposes" sounds like your sales organization's approach, fixing this issue should be prioritized because it negatively affects sales effectiveness. I recommend meeting with sales management, sales enablement, and marketing to create tools, for both during and after the consultation, that will convey message points properly and memorably.

Nonverbals

When sharing information, many salespeople focus exclusively on what they are saying and do not pay enough attention to the DI's nonverbal reactions. It would be nice if DIs provided verbal responses, but there's always more to be learned through their nonverbal signals.

Smiles and head nods are easy reads and tell you the DI likes what they hear. When I notice that, I ask: "I noticed you smiled. What did I say that made you smile?"

I want to know what I said or did that hit the mark with them. It also reinforces my Empathetic Expertise because I am acknowledging their emotions. As you've heard me say before, sales is an open-book test. Don't make it more complicated than it needs to be. Ask questions! Phrased properly, these questions can show you care and are genuinely interested in your DI, and they differentiate you as well.

Conversely, a DI folding their arms or moving away from their desk signify skepticism and doubt about what they've heard. Many salespeople don't notice those signals. Some salespeople notice the behavior but don't address it. A small subset of salespeople will say this:

> **I noticed you moved away from the desk (or folded your arms). What was it that I said that caused you to be uncomfortable?**

By acknowledging their emotional reaction, again, you demonstrate Empathetic Expertise. It shows you care and can quickly turn a negative perception into a relationship-development opportunity. Since you would be among the few salespeople to acknowledge that behavior, you also positively differentiate yourself.

Nonverbal reactions cannot be ignored if these Desired Consultation Outcomes are on your list:

- Gained DI's interest in exploring a relationship with your company.
- Established trust with the DI and took the first steps toward building a relationship.
- Differentiated yourself and provided meaningful value.
- Transitioned the DI's emotions to your intended, desired ones.

Another nonverbal cue is the DI taking notes about what you are saying. Aren't you curious about what they are writing down? You should be. What if you said, "I noticed you've been taking copious notes during our time together. What have I said that piqued your interest?" You'll find that some DIs will then bring up a topic you have not yet discussed. That topic would never have come up without asking this question, meaning an opportunity has been missed.

There is a never-ending list of potential nonverbal responses to the information you share. Watch for those nonverbals. Address them when you notice them and use them as opportunities to build relationships with them.

Storytelling is a skill that can be learned. But learning it is not enough. Salespeople need to master storytelling to energize their deals. *Practice! Practice! Practice!*

I mentioned the delicate balance between sharing too much and too little information during consultations. In the next chapter, you'll learn how to ensure there will be future interactions with the DI and even their colleagues.

THE FIRST MEETING DIFFERENTIATOR: CONCEPT #7

Information sharing through storytelling is a cornerstone of effective consultations, necessitating care in what is shared, when, and how—with the goal of engaging the Decision Influencer and ensuring they remember what you said.

CHAPTER 8

CONSULTATION CLIFFHANGERS
HOW TO GET THEM
TO WANT TO HEAR MORE

n the last chapter, I talked about the delicate balance between sharing too much and too little information during consultations. Too little, and the DI will think you were unprepared and will receive very little meaningful value from the consultation: a deal killer. Too much and the DI may not see a reason to have further meetings because they think they've heard everything. Ensure there is alignment between their expectations and what is delivered during the consultation.

A salesperson's objective is to keep the deal energized and have interactions after the first meeting. But wouldn't it be awesome if, instead, Decision Influencers were the ones pushing to keep the deal moving forward? That can happen if you use a tool I call "Consultation Cliffhangers."

Who Shot J.R.?

When I was eleven years old, one of my favorite television shows was *Dallas*, which featured the trials and tribulations of the oil magnate Ewing family. It was not just something I watched but was a bonding time with my parents, who had hooked me on it.

On March 21, 1980, the producers aired one of the most captivating events in television history when one of the main characters, J. R. Ewing, was shot, but that episode did not reveal who pulled the trigger. This season finale ended without answering the question, "Who shot J.R.?" This mystery became the watercooler talk in most workplaces as everyone tried to solve this whodunit.

The producers used a plot tactic commonly referred to as a cliffhanger. This attention-grabbing strategy's core purpose is to spark enough interest and curiosity that viewers come back to watch the show the following season. Cliffhangers arouse so much emotion that fans can barely wait for the next season. Why does viewership matter to the networks? Viewership drives advertising revenue. The more eyeballs on the screen, the more dollars the network can generate.

This cliffhanger wasn't just a one-time stunt used for this show. Over the years, many television shows (and movies with planned sequels) have used cliffhangers to keep audiences coming back season after season. And this strategy works tremendously well! According to the *New York Daily News*, more than ninety million people in the US, which represented half the televisions in the country, turned their television channels to *Dallas* on November 21, 1980, because they wanted to find out who shot J.R.

From TV to Sales

Salespeople often ask me, "How do I get DIs to meet with me after the first meeting?" They ask this as they develop their consultation strategies and think through the next steps of the process. They seek a response chock-full of words of wisdom. What they receive, however, is a question, "Why should DIs want to meet with you again?" That question is often met with a puzzled look.

Salespeople often struggle with keeping deals energized after the consultation. They try to figure out creative ways to get the DI to agree to a subsequent meeting, but they're focused (discovery mindset) only on their objective, to make a sale. That mindset doesn't work. The focus needs to be on what meaningful value the DIs will receive from subsequent interactions (consultation mindset).

As we've seen, salespeople face a tricky conundrum with consultations. There's a delicate information-sharing balance they need to maintain. They are eager to share everything about their company and what they offer during the first meeting. You may think you told them everything. They may think they heard everything. However, there is a significant issue regarding information-sharing and retention that comes back to the Forgetting Curve I shared in the prior chapter: What will the DI remember?

Plus, once you've shared everything, why should they have future discussions with you? Unless you are in a selling environment where a sale is expected to be completed as part of the consultation, scheduling the next interaction is essential to the deal's success. For a complex, multistep deal that necessitates ongoing conversations to advance it to the finish line, figuring out how to get DIs to agree to future meetings is critical. Additional interactions are crucial also in a repetitive purchasing relationship, where getting together with the DI periodically helps to ensure they continue buying from you.

The mistake many salespeople make during the first meeting, which negatively impacts their ability to schedule future interactions, is to jump into a PowerPoint presentation or a technology demo or to whip out all their product samples. "I have samples of all our materials with me. Let me show you those. I'll now show you our order management system, so you'll know how to order these products, select a shipping option, and manage the status of the orders."

Here's another million-dollar question: If you tell them and show them everything during the first meeting, what reason is there to have another interaction with you? There isn't. Getting them to invest additional time with you will be extremely difficult because you won't have meaningful value to offer in that interaction. And, as Ebbinghaus cited, the DI will forget most of what you shared anyway, so rushing to do it all during the first meeting is a waste of time.

If the nature of your sale is transactional, meaning you are expected to walk out of a consultation with an order, information sharing needs to be comprehensive. However, with a complex, multistep sale, that is not a necessity and actually weakens the deal. Remember the overarching objective of the consultation:

> **Pique a high enough level of interest with Decision Influencers so that they want to continue interacting with you after the consultation.**

Rushing consultations by sharing too much information weakens the deal for two reasons. First, the DI will likely forget what you want them to remember. And second, you spent so much time sharing information, you likely did not ask enough questions.

As I explained in chapter 7, your information-sharing strategy should be based on *what you want the DI to remember, not what you want to tell and show them.* That sentence is so important that I suggest reading it again.

Taking that a step further, you need to share enough information, visually and verbally, during the consultation that the DI is inspired and intrigued to continue a dialogue with you. Determining where that line is varies by salesperson and by deal. The key takeaway is to be mindful of that line.

There are several ways to combat the Forgetting Curve. One is with the consultation structure. During the consultation, create enough value to energize the deal, but don't cover everything so the DI isn't left with the impression that there is nothing more for them to learn from you. What if we were to apply the television cliffhanger strategy to consultations by using a Consultation Cliffhanger?

Consultation Cliffhangers

Just as TV cliffhangers aim to create enough excitement for the audience to come back, Consultation Cliffhangers aim to spark enough interest and curiosity so the DIs want to interact with you again after the first meeting. Consultation Cliffhangers are not accidental. They are a planned part of your overall deal conversion strategy.

Every company and every industry can leverage Consultation Cliffhangers to keep deals energized.

Earlier, I shared the question salespeople asked me about strategies for DIs to agree to having subsequent meetings. How awesome sales would be if after the consultation the DI asked, "When can we get together again?" That absolutely can happen if you strategically use Consultation Cliffhangers!

Here are some Consultation Cliffhanger opportunities. Select only the ones that apply to your selling environment.

Solution Options and Proposal Reviews

During the consultation, you learned about the DI's needs, wants, goals, desires, and objectives. The next step is to create solution options or perhaps a proposal. The easiest way to provide that information is through email. *Never do that!* Easy and effective are not synonymous. Emailing that information encourages ghosting if they don't like what they've read (if they read it at all). A salesperson's goal should always be to have more face time and more interactions with DIs. An in-person meeting is best. But a virtual meeting is also effective.

Solution Options and Proposal Reviews are a Consultation Cliffhanger opportunity enabling you to schedule the next meeting to review the potential solutions you create. In this case, the best approach to schedule the next meeting is to imply acceptance. As you get toward the end of the consultation, say the following:

> Thank you for sharing this information with me today. Where we go from here is for me to work with our team on solution options for you. It'll take a few days to complete that. What is your availability next week to get together and go over the options my team develops?

One possible response from a DI to that question is a request for you to email the options. As I said, *Don't do that!* Proposals are not email interactions. They are conversations. You need their feedback, to see their body language, facial expressions, and overall reaction created. If they ask you to email it, say this:

> Absolutely! Once we walk through the document and make changes to it based on our conversation. There are always questions that come up and changes that get made as we talk through the solutions. Of course, I'll email the final version to you. What is your availability next week to go over this initial version?

You'll notice that I didn't disagree with or agree with their request. I further explained the process and came right back to the availability question. The Solution Options and Proposal Reviews Consultation Cliffhanger is one of the strongest opportunities to schedule additional interactions with the DI.

Research

During consultations, topics may come up that you had not planned to cover, or the DI may ask questions that you don't know the answer to (for example, Beyond Your Pay Grade questions discussed in chapter 4).

Sales 101 tells us never to "wing it." DIs respect salespeople who say something like this:

> **That's a great question, and I know who in my company to ask for the answer. I'll get back to you tomorrow with their response.**

Some salespeople go wrong when they continue in this vein:

> **I'll send you an email with that answer.**

An email is, on rare occasions, the appropriate option if there is a sense of urgency for a fast response. Absent that, researching information is a Consultation Cliffhanger opportunity.

As you get toward the end of your consultation, include this as part of your wrap-up:

> **I'm going to research the answer to your question. What is your availability next week (for a call, a virtual meeting, or an in-person meeting) to go over what I find?**

Boom! You have your next interaction scheduled.

Subject Matter Experts (SMEs)

Most companies have "Yodas" in their organization. These are all-knowing individuals on a particular topic. They are gurus in legal or regulatory compliance, operations, or finance.

Sometimes, a salesperson invites the SME to join them during the first meeting. Three negative results come from this approach. First, the SME does most of the talking, preventing you from asking the essential questions, which weakens the deal's foundation. Second, it's more challenging to schedule subsequent meetings because the DI thinks they have heard everything they need to know about your company and what you offer. And third, the DI won't recall everything that was discussed.

Rather than include the SME in the consultation, use them as a Consultation Cliffhanger. Complete a comprehensive consultation and position the value of your SME to book the next interaction. By having two interactions, the DI will retain more information from each meeting, you have the opportunity to reposition information covered during the first meeting, and the DI can invite others to the next interaction to engage with your SME. Win! Win! Win!

Deals are commonly won by leveraging SME expertise. But it's important to consider how you'll prepare the SMEs. Consider these two options.

First, you could include the SME in the consultation. We've already seen three reasons why this isn't a good idea. In addition, you'll have to uncover a wealth of information during that interaction before the SME can demonstrate meaningful value, making it much more challenging for them to shine on your behalf.

The second option is to share with the SME the information you learned during the consultation so they can prepare for their involvement in the deal. With this approach, the SME can prepare appropriately to dazzle the DI in the next interaction. Of these two options, option two is a no-brainer!

Important! If the DI expects to meet your SME during the consultation, this Consultation Cliffhanger is not appropriate. The DI will be disappointed if you don't bring them. The key is for you not to be the one making the premature overture to include the SME to set the consultation for all the reasons I addressed earlier. Of course, if the only way to book the consultation is by including the SME, do it! But be careful of the pitfalls.

Executive Involvement

Including a member of your executive team can be a helpful component of the deal pursuit strategy. But when do you include them? Rather than at the consultation, have them join in a subsequent interaction. Just like with the SME, if you share information you've acquired during the consultation, your executive can prepare accordingly.

A great way to use this Consultation Cliffhanger is when you recognize that people "north on the organization chart," meaning higher-level executives, will need to be involved for this deal to come together. In other words, if a DI's CFO needs to be involved in future discussions, you can offer to bring along a member of your executive team to the next meeting. Including your executive opens the door for the DI to include their executive(s), which is a second significant benefit to you.

As with the SMEs, don't disappoint them if they expect you to bring an executive to the consultation. But, for the reasons noted above, be very careful when using "executive inclusion" to book a consultation.

Empty Briefcase

Some salespeople sell products and have samples of materials that can be shown. During the consultation, you'll uncover the DI's needs and what materials would be appropriate to share.

One option is to bring all the samples you could possibly need to the consultation. A more effective option, however, is to use the first meeting to identify the right samples for their application. Use "seeing samples" as the reason to schedule the next meeting, which allows the DI to invite others to join the next interaction.

Consider this: If you are in the camp that says "I sell solutions," how can you arrive at a consultation with a bag of solutions? It doesn't make sense. For those salespeople in complex sales that create solutions, consider the Empty Briefcase Strategy Consultation Cliffhanger.

Arrive with nothing but a pad of paper, a pen, and your pre-consultation research notes. The plan is to come to the next meeting with relevant solution options based on the consultation results. This strategy disarms DIs because they don't feel like you've shown up on their doorstep to push a sale. It comes across that you are there to understand them and determine if there is a potential match between the two organizations. If there is a possible match, you will share the appropriate solution during the next interaction. The Empty Briefcase Strategy is also a creative differentiation opportunity that sets a positive tone with DIs.

This Consultation Cliffhanger is not appropriate in all circumstances. If the DI expects to see samples during the consultation, then you need to show them something, a few, but not everything. Remember the delicate balance of too little versus too much.

Technology Demos

Salespeople are so proud of their company's technology, and they should be. If not, why are you selling for that company? But don't let that excitement cause a rushed, incomplete consultation. "Let me show you our online order management system." The consultation will quickly turn into a show-and-tell, and it will fail to create a solid deal foundation because, most likely, all the questions that needed to be asked were not.

As noted in chapter 6, many salespeople are leery of asking too many questions, and, of course, you should consider the optimal number of questions. However, that should not be an issue if you've set the expectation with the DI that your questions are intended to determine whether you have something relevant to offer. Doctors never apologize for asking too many questions during a consultation, nor should you.

What happens all too often is a salesperson asks a few questions and rushes to the show-and-tell demo. Why not make these two distinct interactions? This is an opportunity for a Consultation Cliffhanger. We know the DI will remember only so much of what you share. Scheduling the next interaction advances the deal and allows them to invite others, which is, again, a win for you.

If needed, you can always conduct a brief demo to give the DI a taste and spark curiosity. But the full demo is for meeting two!

Product Demos

Product demos face the same challenge as technology ones: salespeople ask a handful of questions, and then . . . *Boom!* Here comes the full product demo. The consultation suffers as a result. Again, the DI won't remember as much as you would like them to, and scheduling the next meeting will be much more challenging.

If needed, show a little bit of the product to spark intrigue, but don't fall into the trap of conducting a full product demo during the consultation for all the reasons already mentioned.

Updates

The Updates Consultation Cliffhanger has two primary applications. The first is for the complex sale. During the consultation, you learned a wealth of information about them and what the DI seeks to accomplish. Rather than delve into updates regarding trends, regulations, and best practices, use this Consultation Cliffhanger as the reason to meet again. The Updates Consultation Cliffhanger works great in tandem with the SME one.

The second application is for those in sale types for which periodic meetings with DIs are needed to ensure the buying relationship continues or because the deals have longer sales cycles.

Anyone with decision-making responsibilities wants to always be in the know. A way for you to continually provide meaningful value is to meet with them to discuss new trends, regulatory updates, and industry best practices.

These aren't the only Consultation Cliffhangers. There are tons more. The important takeaway for you is to *pace the process*. Don't try to cover too much during the consultation or during any other process step. If the consultation is handled correctly, you will have the opportunity for another interaction, and Consultation Cliffhangers can help you accomplish that.

As a side note, I explained Consultation Cliffhangers to my wife, who works with special education students at our local high school. She asked how she could use this concept with her students. "How about on Friday you tell them about a special *thing* they will do on Monday? Or a treat they are going to receive on Monday?" Don't tell them what it is. Just create intrigue so they are eager to come to school the following week.

Analyze your sales environment and select the appropriate Consultation Cliffhangers to have more DIs desiring further interactions with you.

THE FIRST MEETING DIFFERENTIATOR: CONCEPT #8

Consultation Cliffhangers aim to inspire the Decision Influencers to have additional interactions after the consultation.

CHAPTER 9

THE IMPERFECT CONSULTATION
NAVIGATING FIRST MEETING
DEAL OBSTACLES

B ased on everything you've read thus far, you may think I've laid out a strategy for perfect consultations every time. Oh, if only that were true. I bet you won't have a single consultation where you don't encounter what I call Deal Obstacles. These impediments for a deal moving forward require a specialized approach to resolve them.

In this chapter, you'll learn strategies to navigate the common Deal Obstacles that arise *during consultations*. I emphasized *during consultations* in that last sentence because some Deal Obstacles are not likely to occur during the first meeting. One of those is price balking. In most complex sales, you won't include specific, detailed conversations regarding price in your consultations. Thus it is not within the scope of this book. I do address the pricing Deal Obstacle in *Sales Differentiation* and *Sell Different!* But here, I will focus on those that may occur during consultations.

Deal Obstacle: Withholding Information

The sales world has brought this Deal Obstacle upon itself through years of deceitful practices. Expect Decision Influencers not to trust you during early interactions. Trust is earned. The salesperson is responsible for creating an environment where DIs feel comfortable being open and honest. Failing to create that environment results in flawed consultations. Coming back to the medical metaphor, doctors can't make a correct diagnosis if patients are not forthcoming with information. The same holds true for salespeople. You need DIs to openly share information so you can properly *diagnose* their situation and create a *prescriptive* solution.

As discussed in chapter 6, one reason DIs withhold information lies in how a salesperson sequences their questions. Salespeople have to earn the right to ask sensitive questions. Be mindful of what you ask, when you ask, and how you ask. Too many questions can make the consultation feel like an interrogation, so limit your questions by staying focused on your Desired Consultation Outcomes.

One common yet sensitive topic discussed during consultations is money, particularly when you want to know how much they pay their current supplier. This is a great example of a question you need to earn the right to ask, and when you do, you need to phrase it so they are comfortable sharing the information. An effective way I've found to broach this topic is by saying this:

> **Just curious, what are you paying for that today? I ask because I don't want to excite you about potentially working with us if your current provider is cheaper.**

A lot is going on in those two sentences. It starts with a tool I call an "insulator," a question softener. Insulators like "just curious" help make consultations more conversational and remove the bite from what DIs may perceive as invasive questions.

After asking what they are paying today, without hesitation, you continue by explaining why you are asking this question. This question also exposes if the DI is willing to spend more to have a more robust solution. I'm focusing on price here because I want to understand their perspective on what they are paying for what they are receiving, which is especially important if your solution will likely be a more significant investment. If you are going to lose, lose early!

Deal Obstacle: Skepticism

During consultations, you may encounter a skeptical DI. They may be skeptical about your company, your solution approach, or even their own internal ability to achieve the results you've discussed. Skepticism is a negative emotion that can be a deal killer. As we saw with Empathetic Expertise, the only way deals move forward when skepticism arises is to transition their negative emotions to neutral or positive ones.

A mistake salespeople commonly make when facing skepticism is using the "throwing spaghetti at the wall" strategy to attempt to resolve this concern. "What if we have a pilot program ...?" "What if I send you a case study ...?" "How about I give you a reference to talk with ...?" These approaches don't work because you cannot resolve skepticism unilaterally. When skepticism rears its ugly head, it takes both you and your DI working together to resolve it. This concern can be resolved with E.A.S.E.™, my Deal Obstacle Resolution Framework.

The E.A.S.E. Deal Obstacle Resolution Framework

E = Demonstrate **EMPATHY** for their concern.

A = **ASK** questions to fully understand their concern.

S = **SHARE** relevant information based on your understanding of their concern.

E = **ENSURE** the information you shared resolved their concern.

The first "E" stands for Empathy. Start with an empathetic statement like, "I appreciate your sharing that with me." I cannot overstate the importance of starting the resolution process by making an empathetic statement. It serves two purposes. It shows the DI that you've heard and respected their concern, once again demonstrating your Empathetic Expertise. And it gives you a few seconds to think about the direction in which you will take the conversation.

The second step of the Framework is "A," which stands for Ask. It is impossible to properly navigate any concern without fully understanding the issues surrounding it. You may need one question or several to gain a complete picture of the appropriate information to share to resolve their concern.

In this case, we need the DI to think through the issue with us. As I said earlier, you cannot resolve skepticism unilaterally; it takes both of you to resolve it. A question I've found effective when encountering skepticism is this one:

> **What can we do together that will give you the confidence you need to consider working with us?**

This sets the stage for collaboration. You may wonder why I use the word *consider* rather than asking directly about awarding the deal. It's because this is a questioning strategy to use during a consultation. In consultations, it's premature to directly ask for that level of commitment. The goal is to resolve the DI's early-stage skepticism and to firmly position yourself as a viable option rather than having yourself excluded from consideration.

As mentioned, you may need to ask multiple questions before you gain an understanding of which information to share. If the DI doesn't respond to the initial question, consider asking this one in a follow-up:

> **Would you like me to share with you what helped others in the past, who felt the same way you do, to feel comfortable with *this*?**

I use the word *this* because it is a placeholder for the skepticism issue at hand, which you have yet to fully understand.

If the DI has genuine interest in exploring a relationship with you, that second question can often lead to the brainstorming you need. If these two questions don't lead to a plan to resolve their skepticism, strongly consider whether the deal is worth pursuing further. Remember, if you are going to lose, lose early!

Assuming you've identified ideas to resolve their skepticism, the third step of the Deal Obstacle Resolution Framework is "S," which is for Share. This refers to sharing information to resolve the concern now that you fully understand it.

Based on the follow-up question you asked ("Would you like me to share with you what helped others in the past, who felt the same way you do, to feel comfortable with *this*?"), you would then share information that has helped others, including having a pilot program, reviewing a case study, or talking with a reference. The difference between the E.A.S.E. Deal Obstacle Resolution Framework and the "spaghetti throwing" approach is targeting your response. As a result of E.A.S.E., the DI asks for information that will help them feel comfortable considering you rather than you randomly tossing out ideas, hoping they hit the mark.

The last "E" and final component of this framework stands for Ensure. This question *ensures* the information you share will resolve the DI's concern. Let's say the DI asks for a reference. An example of an Ensure question is as follows:

> **What would you need to hear from our client that would help you feel comfortable considering us?**

Connecting them with a client is not enough to resolve skepticism. You need the DI to think through their conversation with your client and determine what they need to hear from them to feel comfortable with you to a level where they will see your solution as a viable option for consideration. You may also want to consider suggesting some topics for them to bring up with your client.

The E.A.S.E. Deal Obstacle Resolution Framework isn't just for resolving skepticism. It is appropriate for any Deal Obstacles that come up during any sales interaction.

Deal Obstacle: Funding Source

If one of your Desired Consultation Outcomes is "learning the funding source for this initiative," that's also a conversation that requires finesse. What you are trying to understand is how the DI plans to pay for your solution. What is important to keep in mind is the spectrum of reasons a DI agrees to a consultation with you.

At one end of that spectrum is a corporate *mandate*: an executive with a high level of authority is requiring an issue to be addressed. With a mandate, the executive knows an investment is needed to resolve the issue. It may or may not be enough funding, but the executive knows they will have to invest to address the issue.

At the other end of that spectrum is an *idea*. This DI may be exploring an idea to see if it is worthwhile. The idea side of the spectrum is another cause of salespeople chasing deal mirages. In these cases, DIs may be in the early stages of exploration and may not have thought about the source of the dollars they'd need for the investment. Or they may not have the authority to allocate dollars. Salespeople sometimes make a dangerous inference in assuming that if someone accepted a consultation, they have decision-making authority. This flawed assumption can lead to salespeople pursuing deals with a low likelihood of being won and thus to wasted sales minutes. An effective question when a DI appears excited about working with you is this:

> **If this is something you wanted to pursue, how would this initiative be funded?**

Don't just listen to the words. Watch their body language. The less precise they are about the funding source, the more concerned you should be about the likelihood of this deal coming to fruition. You have to be able to visualize the deal award road map.

Deal Obstacle: The Illusion of Decision-Making Authority

During your deal pursuits, you'll encounter DIs who appear to have decision-making power. But don't be fooled. There is a critical question to ask yourself:

> **Does this DI have the AUTHORITY to advance the deal or just the ABILITY to kill it?**

If you want to build a pipeline of genuine deals, during your consultation, determine if the DI you are meeting with has the authority to say YES or just the ability to say NO.

Two titles that often fall into this category are project managers and engineers. This is in no way meant to be offensive to people in those roles. From my experience, DIs in these roles usually don't have the authority to say yes, just the ability to say no. This isn't always the case, but it happens often enough that salespeople need to determine *yes authority* versus *no ability* during the first meeting. That doesn't mean there is an expectation of walking out of the first meeting with a signed deal. But there is a lot of wasted sales time spent having meeting after meeting with DIs who have little ability to affect change within their companies.

Of course, finesse is needed when trying to determine *yes authority* versus *no ability* so you don't offend them. Remember, even if this DI can't award you the contract, they can still kill it. Some questions that help expose this issue include:

- "What conversations have you had with your leadership team regarding the importance of addressing this issue now?" (Since multiple DIs will need to bless any change, knowing the internal perspective regarding the issues can expose their level of influence.)
- "If this is something you wanted to pursue, how would this initiative be funded?" (From the prior section, *idea* versus *mandate*.)
- "What internal process have you used for other initiatives you've implemented?" (This question exposes if they have ever spearheaded an initiative that was ultimately implemented.)

Deal Obstacle: Priority

What you sell is the most important thing in the world to you. In most cases, however, it isn't the most important thing to your DI. It's just something on their list to consider or to do. That's why there are four qualifying Outcomes to consider for your Desired Consultation Outcomes list:

- The priority of this initiative relative to other initiatives and why.
- The DI's current corporate goals/future corporate strategy and how you fit within them.
- The DI's personal goals and how you fit within them.
- The business drivers associated with the identified objectives and issues.

These four Outcomes are all tied to one another. Given the number of projects on a DI's plate at any given time, salespeople need to understand how urgent it is for the DI to address the uncovered issues. Urgency is connected to corporate goals, personal goals, and business drivers associated with those issues.

Business drivers are the issue(s) and potential solution(s) that affect the organization financially. Don't expect DIs to fully understand the business case for the issue(s) you address. It's the salesperson's responsibility to help DIs recognize how urgent it is to resolve the issue. This comes back to the point of you having greater expertise than DIs in the world of potential solutions in your industry and your ability to recognize issues they cannot put off.

Whenever deals are out of alignment with goals and business drivers, deals are in jeopardy of being lost to the status quo. As part of your pre-consultation research, seek to understand the DI's goals and align the direction of the consultation with them. Be prepared to position the business drivers associated with their issues. They need to understand your solution's financial impact, which can motivate them to garner support from other DIs who would need to bless this deal down the road.

Toward the end of the consultation, a great question to ask that exposes the DI's level of priority for addressing this issue(s) is this one:

> **I can only imagine how busy you are. Given everything on your plate and what we've talked about today, where does this issue(s) fall in your priority list to address?**

Never assume that the DI is ready to address the issue now because a conversation has gone well (remember, *inconvenience* versus *problem*). The salesperson needs to talk this through with the DI to avoid being surprised later when the deal stalls out because other issues have greater priority.

When navigating any Deal Obstacle, don't just listen to their words, watch their body language. They need to convince you that there is internal energy for resolving the issue. If not, strongly consider whether or not the deal is worth pursuing further.

Deal Obstacle: Change

Let's be clear about your intent when having consultations. Your goal is to lead DIs down a path where they *change* to buying from you. *Change* is a scary word for most people. Like other Deal Obstacles, change can be a deal killer, especially when it affects others in the organization.

Resolving this concern requires an understanding of basic psychology. When left out of decision-making, people might reject decisions they would have otherwise accepted had they been involved in the decision-making process.

Not all DIs will recognize this. The salesperson needs to introduce the topic with a question like this:

> As you can imagine, this [insert solution] will affect [insert titles]. If I could make a suggestion . . . We have found that including [insert titles] early in the solution development discussion leads to the greatest acceptance of the change. What are your thoughts about inviting them to participate in our next meeting?

This question not only deals with this Deal Obstacle but also creates a Consultation Cliffhanger because it creates an opportunity for the next interaction. It also helps you demonstrate expertise in your solutions and again shows your Empathetic Expertise.

Deal Obstacle: Introduction to Others

According to a Gartner study, six to ten people are involved in B2B decision-making. More often than not, your first meeting is with just one Decision Influencer. A deal only comes together if the most heavily influential DIs give their blessing. I'm frequently asked, "How do I get the DI I had a consultation with to introduce me to the other DIs?"

The answer to that question is a question: Why should they introduce you to the other Decision Influencers?

If you can't answer that question, you now know why you're stuck. Think about why they should introduce you. If the DI is genuinely intrigued by what you offer, they will need your guidance to get it. As their Sherpa, guide them and make recommendations to help them get what they want—not what you want but what they want.

What if you said this:

> **I know you said you're excited about what we offer. You mentioned that your CFO needs to weigh in on this. How would you suggest we bring them into the loop?**

Phrasing it this way shows you are trying to help them get what they want, not forcing a sale to get a fat commission check.

We've just gone through the most common Deal Obstacles you'll encounter during consultations and strategies to resolve them. The final component of the consultation strategy is how to end the interaction, which is shared in the next chapter.

THE FIRST MEETING DIFFERENTIATOR: CONCEPT #9

There is no perfect consultation. Expect to encounter Deal Obstacles and plan strategies to resolve them.

CHAPTER 10

PUTTING A BOW
ON A GREAT FIRST MEETING

My grandfather died when I was two years old. A few years later, my grandmother began dating a Brooklyn Italian gentleman named Frank. He used to joke that he gave up meatballs for matzah balls. I credit Frank for teaching me about the importance of having good manners. He'd say, in a full Brooklyn Italian accent, "It don't cost nothing to have good manners. Open doors. Say please and thank you . . ." Of course, he was exactly right.

Suppose your consultation went tremendously well. During the first meeting, you fully qualified the deal. The DI ate up the differentiators you shared through compelling stories. You effectively navigated the Deal Obstacles the DI shared. You both have action items to complete. The meeting is winding down, and there's some awkwardness about how this interaction should end.

The first step to ending a consultation and leaving a positive impression is to thank them for investing time by meeting with you. I can hear Frank in my head saying, "It don't cost nothing to have good manners." You'd be amazed by how few salespeople thank DIs for meeting with them.

After thanking the DI, ask them this:

> **How did we do today?**

I call this a "blank canvas" question because the DI's response could be anything. I always use this question as I end consultations because it tells me what hit the mark with them. Of course, ask that question only if you believe the DI felt the consultation had gone well.

The desired response is something positive, like "This was a great use of my time. I learned a lot today." Or "This was a very helpful conversation. You've given me a lot to think about." In other words, the DI is saying they received meaningful value from the consultation. That's pure gold because the DI feeling they received meaningful value paves the way for future interactions with you and advances the deal.

The Only Acceptable Conclusion

Following the "blank canvas" question, more work must be done to put a bow on the consultation. There is only one acceptable conclusion for a successful consultation. It doesn't matter what you sell. It doesn't matter who you met with. It doesn't matter how simple or complex what you sell is. Remember your overarching objective:

> **Pique a high enough level of interest with Decision Influencers so that they want to continue interacting with you after the consultation.**

The only acceptable ending to the first meeting is establishing well-defined next steps and having the next interaction scheduled. That could be another consultation, a demo, a group meeting, or a pilot program. But this interaction is not an email exchange or a promise to call you next month. The next steps and interactions need to be clearly identified with dates.

Will you be able to achieve that Outcome every time? Of course not. But with that goal in mind, you are much more likely than not to achieve it.

Some salespeople don't achieve that Outcome because they lack clarity regarding what should happen next. If you don't know what you want, you aren't likely to get it. During your pre-consultation planning, think about the different directions the consultation could go and the possible next steps relative to those paths. Professional salespeople guide DIs through a process that addresses the issues they are experiencing and help them see the pathway to resolution. They are looking for you to lead the way!

There are two common ways salespeople discuss the next steps with DIs:

> **Given our conversation today, what do you see as our next best step?**

or

> **How should we leave the conversation for today?**

These questions make the Decision Influencer feel empowered, which they don't often experience when working with salespeople. But the risk with these questions is that DIs don't necessarily know what to do next. They may suggest a next step that will not likely lead to a deal coming to fruition.

A more effective approach, given your expertise, is for you to make a recommendation.

> **Given what you shared with me today, what I recommend we do next is _____. What are your thoughts?**

You'll find many DIs prefer to be guided by experts and will follow your lead. This is why you need clarity regarding your desired next steps. You must know what you want to happen after the consultation in order to make it happen.

Delivery of the "next steps" message is incredibly important to effectiveness. If you are meek, the DI will likely not follow your recommendation. If you are confident—not arrogant but confident—they are more likely to agree with your plan.

As you near the end of the first meeting, also review the action items you both committed to completing. Action items need due dates. Without dates, they likely won't get done. Agree on firm dates whenever possible.

To put a bow on the first meeting, after thanking them for investing time to meet with you, planning next steps, and reviewing action items, share this message:

> **I know we covered a lot of ground today. Later today, I will send you an email that summarizes our conversation. Look for the subject line "Recap."**

I have never received a negative response to this message in all my years using this strategy. The same holds true for my clients who use this approach. This message is always met with appreciation by the DI.

"Just One More Thing"

That's the famous expression of Columbo, the 1970s television detective. A little more juice can be squeezed out of the consultation, such as a referral to other parts of the company (if that is relevant to your sale). Consider this approach:

> One more thing. Given what you now know about who we are and what we offer, if you were me, who else in your company would you reach out to? [Then, after hearing their recommendation:] Would you mind introducing me to them?

The goal is not just to get a name but to have the DI introduce you to them. Why wouldn't they do that, given the great experience they just had with you? Will everyone agree to do this? No. But if you don't ask, you don't get!

If you feel it is appropriate and you've earned the right, ask the question as a referral request outside the organization. Again, you have to earn the right before asking for these introductions. Here are three ways to phrase a request for external referrals.

1. "Given your role as [insert title], I'm guessing you are connected with other [insert title]. If you were me, how would you go about meeting more [insert title] like you?"
2. "You've been working with us for quite a while, so you are familiar with the breadth of what we offer and the quality that we offer. If you were me, how would you go about meeting more [insert title] like you?"
3. "You've been working with us for a while now, so you've seen firsthand the quality and value we bring. I'm always looking to connect with more [insert title] who could benefit from

what we do. If you were in my shoes, how would you go about meeting them?"

Wrapping Up the Consultation

Let's put the pieces together to put a bow on your consultation. Finish it using this sequence:

1. "Thank you for investing time with me today."
2. "How did we do?" (With a positive response, continue.)
3. "Given what you shared with me today, what I recommend we do next is _____. What are your thoughts?"
4. "Based on what we discussed, here's what I need to do." (Action items with agreed-upon due dates.)
5. "Here's what you said you will do." (Action items with agreed-upon due dates.)
6. "I know we covered a lot of ground today. Later today, I will send you an email that summarizes our conversation. Look for the subject line 'Recap.'"
7. "One more thing. Given what you now know about who we are and what we offer, if you were me, who else in your company would you reach out to?" [Then, after hearing their recommendation:] "Would you mind introducing me to them?"
8. "I look forward to our next conversation."

The Finishing Touch

I first presented the concept of the Recap Email in my book *Sell Different!*, and innumerable readers have shared their success with that strategy. A key to success in writing Recap Emails is the quality of the notes you take during the consultation. To continue with the doctor metaphor, doctors document consultations to a level where they capture all pertinent information. They don't expect to remember the details of every consultation. That's the purpose of their note-taking.

Suppose you had a one-hour consultation; the Forgetting Curve tells us DIs will remember about six minutes of the meeting content a week later. That is, unless you send an email that includes the meeting's essential points. That's just one of the benefits the Recap Email provides salespeople. It gives you a second chance to highlight the points you want the DI to remember. Coming back to the two primary reasons why people go to the doctor: to become wiser about the issues they are experiencing and to understand its potential remedies. The Recap Email is the prescriptive summary of the consultation experience for your DI.

The Recap Email also differentiates you. Most salespeople won't bother doing it because it takes work. By providing this, you come across as a true sales professional; you stand out and make a positive impression. There's an old expression regarding salespeople, "What you experience before the sale is an indication of what you will receive after it." The Recap Email sets a positive tone for what it would be like to work with your company because you are a reflection of how your company treats its clients.

Unfortunately, AI tools can't write this for you. It is a manual process, and your DI will know that you took time to write this for them. Recap Emails show you genuinely care (Empathetic Expertise) about them and their success.

The Recap Email also helps keep your deal on track by listing action items and due dates. Think about the number of times you've arrived for a follow-up meeting expecting an update on their action items only to learn they forgot about them. "Oh, that's right, I was supposed to get that report from Operations. Sorry, I forgot." Now, the sales cycle has become protracted.

The Recap Email should have five components: Your Objectives (meaning the DI's stated objectives), How We Can Help, My Action Items, Your Action Items, and Next Steps. Below are the best practices for each of those components.

Your Objectives

- List the challenges and objectives the DI shared along with the reasons they said those needed to be addressed. Use the DI's language when referencing their goals, challenges, and objectives so they feel you've truly heard them. You want them to nod their head in agreement as they read the email.

- Highlight who is impacted by those issues, the actions taken to address them thus far, and the results of those actions.

- Describe the DI's issues with appropriate emotion words that align with the emotions you observed. Emotion drives action!

- Never bad-mouth the competition but empathize with the DI for their current frustrations.

- Share the DI's stated vision for a potential solution with your company.

- Remind them of the urgency needed to address the identified issues (problems, not inconveniences).

How We Can Help

- Include only relevant information rather than everything your company offers. What you share depends on the issues addressed in the "Your Objectives" portion of the email.

- Remind the DI of the differentiators you shared and why they matter. Correlate the differentiators with their stated objectives.

- Share your company overview sound bite to establish credibility. It should be no longer than a paragraph or bullet point summarizing your company's expertise.

- Explain why your company is the right choice given their objectives, but avoid using superlative words like *best* and *expert* (unless it can be proven). Create a sense of urgency for the solution relative to their objectives.

- Include your recommendations and why they are the right approach based on what you learned during the consultation.

- Include any attachments that you identified would be appropriate when you developed your consultation strategy. For example, if you felt you need to share a case study, include that in the email.

My Action Items

- List what you committed to doing and by when.

Your Action Items

- List what they committed to doing and by when.

Next Steps

- List what both you and the DI agreed to as the next steps, including the next scheduled interaction.

When writing this email, use bullet points because they are easier to read.

Most business-to-business sales involve multiple DIs. You met with one, which means the others are uninformed about what you offer. Write the Recap Email so it's easy to share with these other DIs. Your Recap Email can also pique the interest of the other DIs in exploring a relationship with you.

Before hitting the send button, take these two steps:

1. Read it out loud to make sure it conveys the message you intend. For example, if it comes across as arrogant, all your great work will become a DI turnoff.
2. Spell and grammar check the email because message quality reflects on both you and your company. A sloppy email conveys that your company, you, and what you sell are sloppy.

As a best practice, send this email the same day as the consultation because it will be fresh in both your and their minds. The key is to meet the expectations you have set. If you commit to providing the email today, don't miss that commitment! That email must be in their inbox because, again, it reflects on you and your company.

A well-written Recap Email will take about fifteen minutes to complete, but I've never found a salesperson who felt it was not time well invested.

THE FIRST MEETING DIFFERENTIATOR: CONCEPT #10

Effective consultations finish with defined next steps and scheduled subsequent interactions, and they include Recap Emails to keep deals moving forward.

CHAPTER 11

IMPLEMENTING THE FIRST MEETING DIFFERENTIATOR STRATEGY

'␣ve just taken you on a journey to create masterful consultations. In writing this book, my goal has been to inspire you to shift your first meeting mindset from discovery to consultation. I've provided you with a comprehensive, step-by-step guide to implement this mindset to create outstanding first meeting experiences.

Is there a lot of work involved in implementing this strategy? Absolutely. Will it lead to you winning more deals? No doubt!

Let's think of this strategy implementation in terms of phases and plan for phase one.

■

THE FIRST MEETING DIFFERENTIATOR STRATEGY IMPLEMENTATION—PHASE 1

- *Step 1:* Select one type of Decision Influencer to focus on for the development of your first meeting strategy. This should be an individual with whom you most commonly have first meetings.

- *Step 2:* Select one solution you sell to give the strategy a distinct focus.

- *Step 3:* Identify the meaningful value that that DI will receive during a consultation with you. (See chapter 1.)

- *Step 4:* Create your Desired Consultation Outcomes list for a first meeting with that DI. (See chapter 2 and download the worksheet at www.ConsultationOutcomes.com.)

- *Step 5:* Develop a Target Client Profile for the selected solution. (See chapter 3 and download the worksheet at www.TargetClientProfile.com.)

- *Step 6:* Conduct a Decision Influencer Analysis for the selected DI. (See chapter 4 and download the worksheet at www.DecisionInfluencerAnalysis.com.)

- *Step 7:* Conduct an Other Players Analysis for the three most common ones you encounter. (See chapter 4 and download the worksheet at www.OtherPlayersAnalysis.com.)

- *Step 8:* Based on your Desired Consultation Outcomes and Target Client Profile, define the research you will conduct before each consultation. (See chapter 4.)

- *Step 9:* The Decision Influencer Analysis helped you identify the issues your selected solution can address for this DI. The next step is to understand how and why the DI feels about each issue before a consultation with you. Then identify the emotions you want the DI to feel about those issues after the interaction with you to develop your Empathetic Expertise. (See chapter 5 and download the worksheet at www.EmpatheticExpertise Workshop.com.)

- *Step 10:* Based on your Desired Consultation Outcomes, develop Challenge Horizontal Questions and Positioning Horizontal Questions to use during the first meeting. (See chapter 6.)

- *Step 11:* Based on your Desired Consultation Outcomes, create three stories related to your selected solution to share during the first meeting. (See chapter 7.)

- *Step 12:* Select your Consultation Cliffhangers to ensure future interactions with the DI and their organization. (See chapter 8.)

- *Step 13:* Prepare your approach to navigate Deal Obstacles that could arise during the consultation. (See chapter 9.)

- *Step 14:* Create your Recap Email template to send after consultations. (See chapter 10.)

Once you've gone through these steps, you are well on your way to conducting great consultations with this selected DI regarding this solution. But don't stop at phase one. As time permits, further the strategy beyond that one scenario and develop others for

- each DI with whom you conduct consultations and
- each solution your company offers.

Define Desired Consultation Outcomes for each DI relative to each solution. Develop Target Client Profiles for each solution you offer. Conduct additional Decision Influencer and Other Player Analyses. Develop Empathetic Expertise for each DI. Create more solution stories. All of this will be time well invested.

Final Thoughts

As shared in chapter 1, buyers despise discovery experiences because they don't receive meaningful value from them. But they do appreciate well-facilitated consultations. From my years working with individual salespeople and overall sales organizations, I saw a genuine need for assistance with this critical component of the new client acquisition process, which is why I wrote this book.

Once you've created your consultation strategy, document it in a sales playbook that the entire sales organization can use. You can learn more about sales playbooks at www.MyCustomSalesPlaybook.com.

The effectiveness of your consultation strategy should be regularly evaluated with the goal of continuous improvement. After each consultation, introspectively assess it to identify what worked well, what worked somewhat well, and what flopped. Fix the flops and improve the "somewhat wells."

As my clients know, I love hearing about their success stories. You'll find my contact information on the bio page of the book. Shoot me an email. Reach out on LinkedIn. I want to hear from you!

Have a question about implementing my consultation strategy? I'll gladly answer it.

If you are looking for assistance beyond that, including custom sales playbook development, my firm, Sales Architects®, offers consulting, coaching, workshops, and keynote talks based on The First Meeting Differentiator strategy. Learn more at SalesArchitects.com.

I look forward to hearing of how you successfully *win more deals at the prices you want*®!

INDEX

ABOUT THE AUTHOR

LEE SALZ is an internationally renowned sales management strategist, bestselling author, and award-winning speaker specializing in building world-class sales forces. He has worked with hundreds of companies in various industries and sizes to create marketplace disruption by leveraging his Sales Differentiation® strategies—leading to explosive, profitable growth. In 2022, the Institute for Sales Excellence named Lee speaker of the year. In 2025, Global Gurus named Lee to their Top 30 Sales Thought Leaders, ranking him as the #6 sales thought leader in the world.

Lee is a sales contrarian who combats old-school, ineffective selling methods and challenges you to think differently about your sales approach. He has written six bestselling business books, including *Sales Differentiation* and *Sell Different!*, which have been called the "one-two punch" every salesperson needs to differentiate what and how they sell to *win more deals at the prices you want*®.

A featured columnist in *The Business Journals* and a media source on sales and sales management, Lee has been quoted and featured in the *Wall Street Journal*, CNN, *The New York Times*, MSNBC, ABC News, and numerous other outlets.

Lee is a frequently sought keynote speaker at sales meetings, association conferences, and virtual events. He also conducts customized workshops on a wide array of sales performance topics.

A graduate of Binghamton University, originally from New York City and New Jersey, Lee now resides with his family in Minneapolis. When Lee isn't working with clients to help them *win more deals at the prices you want*®, you'll find him in the gym. He is a champion powerlifter in the bench press.

Lee can be reached at lsalz@salesarchitects.com for consulting, coaching, workshops, and keynote talks, which are available in both in-person and virtual formats. You can also follow him on all the major social media platforms.